A Spade is Still a Spade:

Essays on Crime and The Politics of Jamaica

Bernard Headley

LMH Publishing Limited

Cover Design by: Susan Lee Quee

Edited by: Barbara Hall

Book Design & Typeset by: Michelle M. Mitchell

Published by: LMH Publishing Limited
7 Norman Road,
LOJ Industrial Complex,
Building 10,
Kingston C.S.O., Jamaica.
Tel: 876-938-0005; 938-0712
Fax: 876-759-8752
Email: lmhbookpublishing@cwjamaica.com
Website: www.lmhpublishingjamaica.com

Printed in the U.S.A.   ISBN   976-8184-36-1

The thing that's needed is to inflame the civic temper as past history has inflamed the military temper.

—William James, *The Moral Equivalent of War*

Preface

Reported levels of *all* crime and violence in Jamaica have indeed reached crisis proportions. The official crime numbers—let alone the countless but unrecorded anecdotes and horror stories of victimisations—describe a society under siege by crime. The crimes run the entire gamut: from common property crimes to fraud, racketeering, and corruption in high places. But most worrisome to all sectors of the society have been the extraordinarily high numbers of homicides.

Over the last four or so years, annual homicide rates in Jamaica averaged in the vicinity of 40 or more murders per 100,000 inhabitants, placing Jamaica near the top of countries with the highest murder rates in the world. The record-high number of murders between 1999 and 2001 (over 2,760), plus the sheer horror in several killings, have suggested to local authorities, and the news media, that a far more "evil" force than either ordinary criminality or violent personal conflicts is working to undermine the country's social order. At root, threatening the stability of the nation, so officials within the nation's National Security regime have warned, is a terrorist menace, particularly the menace of narco-terrorism.

With Jamaica having in recent years become a key transshipment point for much of the illegal drugs entering the United States and Great Britain, this has pushed conventional criminal activity in the island into a whole other realm, according to the Minister of National Security, Dr. Peter Phillips. The high homicide numbers is the most glaring manifestation of this troubling new dimension, Phillips has repeatedly argued.

But, curiously, the Jamaican police's own homicide data hardly confirm the view of a narco-terrorist menace. Of the 887 murders committed in 2000, the police attributed less than 13 per cent to "drug and gang-related activity," to use the police's rather imprecise designation. The greater numbers were for robbery (25 per cent) and for domestic and reprisal killings (32 and 33 per cent, respectively). A similar trend holds for the huge 1,139 murders committed in 2001.

And, to take it a step further, of the more than 500 murders reported for the first six months of 2002, less than 12 per cent have been linked to so-called "gangs and drugs".* Unknown portions of these "gangs-and-drugs" homicides for the years 2000, 2001, and early 2002, then, might easily have been related to usual gang activity *only*—having to do with politics or other non-drug conflicts—leaving a similarly unknown but certainly smaller number relating specifically to drugs. In other words, the overwhelming number of all homicides in the country has had more to do with domestic and other inter-personal and inter-group conflicts, than with narcotics trafficking.

This is not to say that a serious illegal drug-market problem, with its inherent tendency toward extreme violence, does not now exist in and is not harming the entire country. Indeed, Jamaican drug gangs (or posses) are widely known for the brutal, fierce energy that they bring to the international trade in narcotics. Still, what they are engaged in is nothing more threatening than crimi-

---

* Contrast this with the situation in for example, the District of Columbia, in the U.S., where since the late 1980s more than 60 percent of all killings have been directly drug related.

nality, taken perhaps to a new *criminal* level; but still representing nothing more unusual or exotic than the same old "spade."

Redefining the drug gangs' activities as "something else," as terrorism, not only confuses the issue: it also circumvents the root problem of crime and a pervasive culture of violence in the society. The causes of, and the solutions for, crime and violence are not one and the same for terrorism—though admittedly they are not mutually exclusive.

In mid-January 2002, right after Minister Peter Phillips announced to the nation his plan for dealing with the nation's seemingly untameable crime problem, the editors of *The Sunday Gleaner* asked me to do an op-ed piece articulating a critique (along lines just set forth) of the Minister's "crime plan." The response to the piece evoked a wide range of responses, prompting three additional pieces. Readers—particularly students—urged that I bring all four together in one central place. They appear here (after considerable revisions) as the first four chapters. Two other essays approach from two different angles the problem of law enforcement in a pluralistic society. I present in the final chapter the full text of a "brief" that a government-appointed Commission of Enquiry into the violent events of July 7-10, 2001, in West Kingston, asked me to submit. I especially include it here because it attempts to clarify, from the vantage point of recent history, the characteristics of the kind of social order created that has impacted the nature of much urban crime and violence in Jamaica.

Acknowledgements

Much appreciation to editors Garfield Grandison and Phyllis Thomas of the Jamaica *Gleaner* for receiving, critiquing, and editing the five original essays that have been revised and now re-appear here, after even more revisions. Special thanks to Mavis Belasse and her staff of *The Gleaner's* photographic and copyrights department for digging through what I imagine must have been mounds of material to locate and reproduce my requested items. I especially appreciate also the interest and expertise of staff of LMH Publishing. They were a pleasure to work with every step of the journey towards final production of this modest volume.

Contents

Terrorists, Narco- Terrorists, & Posses

Box 1

100 Lane massacre — Two children, three women, two men shot dead

By Leonardo Blair, Staff Reporter

Seven people, two young children among them, were yesterday slain in a midnight massacre by some 30 gunmen in the 100 Lane community off Red Hills Road . . .

In the deadly rampage, which lasted for more than an hour, five females including two schoolgirls, and two men, were cut down. Police said it was the latest episode in a simmering feud between some residents of 100 Lane and Parke Lane, which are linked by a narrow alley just a few metres long.

According to the police, the feud was rekindled on New Year's Eve when gunmen, allegedly from 100 Lane, murdered Glenroy Maize, 32, juice vendor, of Parke Lane, and wounded four other persons . . .

Deputy Supt. James Forbes, head of he Constabulary Communications Network, said the massacre began just after midnight and when it ended there were seven bodies in the community . . The bodies of Oneil 'Junior' Sammuels, 24, and Edlesha 'Bubba' Montgomery, 18, were charred, as were their goats, when their shacks were set ablaze after the gunmen shot them up with AK 47 and M 16 assault rifles and semi-automatic handguns.

Also killed were six-year-old Shakerra Malcolm, her 11-year-old sister, Tanesha Wilson, their mother Marlene 'Doreen' James, 33; and Rudy "Gutty Ranks" Wilson, 28, who were all cut down in a barrage of bullets which rattled their wooden houses.

Along a pathway from 100 Lane, Andrea Simmonds, 33, a bartender, was executed by the sporadic spurt of bullets, her body forming a shield which apparently enabled her son, Sujay, eight, to survive.

Residents say her life might have been spared if it had not been for the angry order from a gunman who ordered a crony of his to 'shoot the . . . gal!'

after he had initially spared her life. He then pumped several bullets into the body of the pleading woman.

Grief was etched on the face of 13-year-old Ricardo Wilson, who lost his two sisters and mother in the ghastly attack.

Still frightened and shocked, he hardly cried. "Mi just feel weak. Mi father did tell mi mother say the lane no look right but through she is a Christian, she just pray, pray, pray and never say nutten," he said.

If Ricardo had slept at his mother's house that night chances are he could have been dead too. "Is just through me disrespect mi father and mi never 'pologise why mi did deh ah mi auntie," he said.

The attack has left residents of both Parke Lane and 100 Lane in fear and there was an exodus of residents up to late yesterday evening. Residents of 100 Lane claimed that a gang of more than 30 men invaded the inner-city community from neighbouring Parke Lane and that some of the killers came from other areas as well.

The deaths of the seven would be avenged, some said . . .

The 100 Lane residents claim that the men wore trench coats and had caused a blackout in the area by shooting up an electrical transformer before the attack.

In Parke Lane, some persons who say they could not afford to move out, were adamant that they would not be running away from 'no gunman'. They said it was the 100 Lane men who triggered off the war . . .

It is said the murder of Glenroy Maize in Parke Lane had been in reprisal for the stabbing of a man from 100 Lane a few days before New Year's Eve.

The attack on Parke Lane reportedly by men from 100 Lane occurred around midnight by eight men reportedly wearing blue denim and military fatigues, and armed with handguns and rifles . . .

Excerpted and reprinted with permission,
The Gleaner, *Friday, January 4, 2002*

Off the mark [f]

I n civil democracies, government is expected to perform two key functions. The first is to secure the physical borders of the state—its land, sea, and air. And the second is to provide adequately for the public safety of its citizens. In well-functioning democracies, average citizens will hardly feel compelled to bother about knowing how many vessels are patrolling the nation's coastline at any given moment, the condition of those vessels, or the kind of technical equipment sea and airport authorities have at their disposal.

They will feel no special reason to worry over the minutiae in such matters because that's what they pay their elected officials and civil servants to do. The ordinary citizen will then go to sleep at night assured that a responsible government will, in the course of its normal and routine administration of the affairs of the state, maintain at full capacity the nation's vital security assets. And that it will be constantly receiving,

[f] Revised and reprinted with permission, *The Gleaner* (January 20, 2002)

and acting on, advice of experts on matters of modernisation and technical improvement. Hardly do mundane matters relating to things like scanning equipment and vessel horse-power rise to the level of political discourse.

Government, citizens will moreover expect, will go about implementing, as needed, strategic change in security operational procedures without unduly interfering in their normal or everyday lives. Unless, that is, the government of the day can convincingly demonstrate, and irrefutably specify, the imminence of some cataclysmic threat to the state; and that the level of its interference is proportionate to the magnitude of the threat.

The "Threat"

No right-thinking Jamaican would dare argue that crime, disorder, and general breakdown are not overarching threats to the nation and society. However, the P. J. Patterson-led People's National Party (PNP) government's analysis of these variegated phenomena misses the mark considerably. While I have no quarrel with the government's plan to improve technologically its national security apparatus and to implement a 'Peace Management Initiative', I find objectionable several of its proposed measures for fighting so-called 'terrorism', especially since the powers that be have not unequivocally demonstrated the existence of any such threat.

Yet, from the moment Patterson picked him in late 2001 for the job of Minister of National Security, to replace the embattled K. D. Knight, 'terrorism' is essentially what Minister Peter Phillips has been calling Jamaica's crime problem.

In public speeches and on radio talk shows, Phillips has been linking the country's inordinately high levels of urban crime and violence to what he refers to as 'narco-terrorism'. (Some 1,139 persons were murdered in 2001, and the police have recorded more than 500 such deaths for the first half of 2002).

This particular brand of 'terrorism' Phillips and his government have presented as a looming threat—of terrible, catastrophic proportions—to Jamaica's well being and national security. Crime, violence, urban decay, and breakdown of one kind or another have all been reified as, and reified into, Osama bin Ladenesque terrorism.

In an address on April 24, 2002, to participants in a seminar on "anti-money laundering," held at the Jamaica Conference Centre, Phillips explained why the Jamaican government was flexing its muscles over the trade in illegal drugs. He noted that Jamaica was increasingly becoming a transhipment capital for illegal drugs, pointing out that, 'over the past several months some 100 to 120 tonnes of cocaine was shipped through Jamaica'. Of this, some 40 tonnes was destined for Europe, while the remainder was destined for the United States. He also highlighted that the same conduits for illegal drugs were also used for trafficking weapons. He reported that the proceeds of this trade were used to finance and sustain drug lords and cartels. He further pointed out that illegal drugs represented a U. S. 500-billion-dollar industry worldwide. This, the Minister said, was nearly double the size of the global pharmaceutical industry, and nearly ten times the size of global development assistance.

The government's main solution, as put to the nation by

Phillips in a televised broadcast on January 17, would be several far-reaching, tough law enforcement measures, topped off by extraordinarily stiff penalties for drug traffickers. In addition, there would be greater involvement of the police and military in the lives of law-abiding citizens.

To directly confront the terrorist threat, the government's 12-point 'crime plan' (Box 2) stipulated that the security forces (i.e., the police and military) would be conducting more joint operations than heretofore. They would be carrying out more patrols, spot checks, roadblocks, curfews, and cordons. And they would be receiving from Great Britain a number of armoured vehicles and other heavy-duty offensive equipment, the type the Brits had used in fighting *their* terrorists—the Irish Republican Army (IRA).

The Jamaican government under Phillips' initiative is using, in my reasoned opinion, what amounts to one heck of a sledgehammer to smash only a medium-sized fly. It's a worrying, discomfiting fly, yes; but it's a fly that is stuck in a jar filled with a far more insidious and noxious 'ointment'.

The political opposition's response to Minister Phillips' crime plan—as well as its own crime proposals—was even more convoluted, at least for a while. Opposition Jamaica Labour Party (JLP) Leader Edward Seaga initially called for wider application of the death penalty statute for drug crimes. Convicted 'drug dons', Seaga challenged, should be executed by the state.

Seaga would within days of making this hasty, ill-thought-out pronouncement publicly retract it—after attempts at clarrification were largely unsuccessful and many in his camp, and the larger public, found it shocking and disheartening. His point, though—i.e., to challenge pro-death penalty thinking about who else, other than marauding gardeners and girlfriend killers, should swing from the nation's gallows—was probably a valid one. Why not also have swinging partisan-affiliated drug barons?

(c) The Gleaner Co.Ltd

Armoured cars from Great Britain; the kind the Brits used in fighting their terrorists—the Irish Republican Army.

Stuck in a Muck

My contention is that the nature of the official discourse—led by the government and perhaps to a lesser extent the opposition—on the illegal drug trade problem in Jamaica has the tendency to ignore or overlook a number of fundamental realities. When closely examined, these realities suggest some profound implications as to the real reasons behind Jamaica's serious drug trade problem in the first place. They also unmask the true nature of Jamaican involvement in narcotics trafficking and challenge core assumptions about the kind of solutions being proffered.

Four essential realities underscore the nature of Jamaican engagement in international narcotics trafficking:

1. The large-scale presence of a desperate population in search of economic opportunities.
2. Because of Item 1, official deterrent measures can, at best, only be marginally effective at reducing the trade in illegal drugs.
3. The prevalence of a few well-connected drug barons who have been mainstreamed into the business and political upper reaches of the society complicates as it frustrates suppression of the drug 'industry'.
4. Narcotic trafficking in the country is not, for all intents and purposes, organized around terrorist themes, issues, or causes.

Merely coincidental to Jamaica's emergence as a transshipment point for the trade in illegal drugs is its strategic Caribbean location; that is, inside major shipping lanes and air routes between the drug-producing countries of South America and the large drug-consuming nations in Europe and North America. More critical to that emergence has been the steady progression, inside Jamaica, of particular forces that are essential to the support system of significant narcotics trafficking. Added to location have been at least two generations of a displaced *lumpen* proletariat—armies of surplus, dispossessed young people, male and female, who since the end of the 1960s have constituted a quarter of the population of the Kingston Metropolitan Area (Lacey 1977).

Like everyone else in the society, they seek economic opportunities—ideally legal opportunities. But they are not un-willing, in the face of closed or nonexistent legal avenues, to seek recourse within an illegal or a 'hustling' opportunity struc-ture—be it operating an illegal taxi or 'arbitrary vending' in the middle of downtown city streets.

With little in their own existence worth living for, but with babies to feed, many will hardly think twice about risking life and limb (like packing their stomachs with packets of co-caine for trans-oceanic flights) to move drugs from Colum-bia into the rich U. S. and British markets. An earlier genera-tion did much the same with homegrown ganja.

A desperate situation like this renders almost meaning-less solutions that are primarily oriented toward 'improved' law enforcement and apprehension. An effective law enforce-ment apparatus and criminal justice system can only at best apprehend—and maybe punish—a tiny fraction of the mass of actual and potential *motivated* offenders within the soci-ety. For both groups, greater threats of apprehension and punishment bring recalculation or doubling of efforts to minimise risks, to reduce endangerment to what it is they figure they simply have to do. So, as the recent past has shown, if the authorities move the football farther down field, for easier striking or scoring distance against a disaffected population, desperate and determined 'players' that the poor are, they will not simply get fed up and walk off the field. Rather, they will regroup, reconfigure, and reconstitute; be-cause 'today *fi yu*, tomorrow *fi mi*'.

The goal of suppressing the illegal drug trade in Jamaica is equally compromised, though, by its control and coordination at the top by drug kingpins and/or 'dons', who are also well integrated into the country's political and business mainstream. Their numbers are small—but significant (police sources estimate the number of dons, of all 'types' [1], in the Kingston area to be around 25). Leading drug dons who are recognized in polite society as successful businessmen typically channel, through money laundering, cash drug payments into their legitimate, often government-contracted business enterprises.

Still, they are, figuratively, little, pint-sized men—these Jamaican kingpins. They neither own nor command fearsome renegade battalions. Neither are they in league with insurrectionary, rebel leaders, as were drug barons Carlos Lehder and Pablo Escobar in Columbia. If only the Jamaican government could—or would—really 'go after' its local drug kingpins. It would, in all likelihood, diminish the country's narcotics trade problem.

And then, perhaps, the nation could get on with attending to the underlying problems in the society that lie at the root of all crime, particularly gruesome, everyday murders, like the ones that occurred at 100 Lane and Parke Lane in Red Hills, in north central urban St. Andrew (Box 1), which have nothing to do with 'narco-terrorism'. What happened at Parke Lane and 100 Lane were terrifying *crimes*, but they were not acts of terrorism—a key issue I will turn to in the next three chapters.

Box 2

*Excerpts from The Government's
Crime Plan**

Border Control

First priority is to tighten control over Jamaica's borders to plug the holes through which the drugs, guns, and ammunition flow.

To this end, legislation is being developed to enforce greater control over access to air and seaports and to set more stringent standards for port operators.

A team left the island . . . to review x-ray technologies, to allow for the electronic and physical inspection of all cargo coming through our air and seaports. Steps have already been taken to secure closed surveillance equipment for this purpose.

In order to enhance our in-shore and offshore patrol and interdiction capability, the Jamaica Defence Force Coast Guard will shortly receive three new-high-speed marine patrol vessels and efforts are underway to identify other craft as well for the Marine Police.

In addition, negotiations are underway to secure coastal surveillance, radar equipment to facilitate interdiction efforts by the Combined Security Forces and their foreign partners.

Immediately, we will be strengthening the Immigration Department, supplying new data processing and information technologies to apprehend foreign criminal elements who seek to use Jamaica to carry out their criminal activity.

Drug Traffickers Scan

With foreign assistance, we are acquiring IONSCAN equipment and associated technical support to detect and apprehend drug traffickers moving in and out of the country.

Money Laundering

The Money Laundering Act will be amended and strengthened to plug existing loopholes and among other things, broaden the mandatory requirement for reporting suspicious money transactions.

Manpower

In the short-term, any effort to bring in the guns and create a more peaceful atmosphere in the communities will require more security personnel.

There is to be a major recruitment effort to fill these 3,000 vacancies between the Jamaica Defence Force, Jamaica Constabulary Force and Island Special Constabulary Force, and to provide training.

Crime Fighting

The Commissioner of Police and the Chief of Staff have been instructed to immediately develop fighting response capabilities to rapidly confront the terrorist challenge, wherever it occurs in Jamaica. This will involve joint operations by military and police personnel. The Security Chiefs have already begun to review their land, air, and sea tactics. Also in this regard, I have requested international assistance and advisers from friendly countries with experience in fighting urban terrorism. This response capability will be in addition to the crime fighting functions of the Crime Management Unit.

A number of armoured vehicles and other crime fighting equipment will arrive in the island this month to assist the Security Forces in the battle to take back our communities from the criminals and terrorists.

Peace Management

Launch of Peace Management Initiative involving the political parties, the Church, civic organisations, musicians, the University of the West Indies and non-government agencies . . .

*Excerpted from "Gov't Outlines Plans to Fight Crime" [presented by National Security Minister Peter Phillips], The Gleaner, Thursday, January 17, 2002

2

Terrorism as war, not criminality*f*

Sixteen recommendations were set forth in the well-thought-through Report of the National Committee on Crime and Violence, released to the public in October 2001 by the Government of Jamaica (2001). Prime Minister P. J. Patterson had appointed the Committee of noteworthy citizens, in both business and government, to look into the root causes behind a shattering spate of violence that racked parts of downtown Kingston from late April through late July 2001. Because the work of the Committee was distinctly non-partisan (or at least bi-partisan), its recommendations have been greeted favourably by the leadership of the ruling People's National Party (PNP) and the opposition Jamaica Labour Party (JLP)—a well received respite in the nation's struggle against an insistent nightmare.

---

f Revised and reprinted with permission, *The Gleaner* (February 10, 2002)

One seemingly trivial area of concern, which the Committee nevertheless thought important to call attention to, was the matter of definition. The Committee, it seems, wanted the government to be clear on exactly how it was defining aspects of the crime problem, insisting thereby that wrong or overdrawn definitions can only further complicate and may even worsen what it is the country is collectively trying to deal with.

Take the matter of "terrorism" and its corollary "narco-terrorism". The definition of terrorism that Committee members apparently liked was one given in the September 22, 2001, edition of *The Economist* magazine, which they quoted in their report. "Terrorism," reads the quotation, is a "horribly calculated attempt to use violence to help achieve an objective." By this "general standard," according to the Committee, "at least some criminal acts taking place in Jamaica may be said to be terrorist in intent and nature." The Committee cautioned, however, "against the rhetoric in a direction that enlarges the problem or further damages the image of the country, particularly where national security risks are not clearly evident . . . " (Government of Jamaica 2001, p. 29)

Are both the government's and the opposition's conceptualisation of the nation's crime problem, then, as a war against terrorism (or "type of terrorism") correct? What if that conceptualisation were wrong? Would the government and political opposition then not, together, be falsely enlarging the problem, frightening away even more visitors and potential investors? And more gravely, what kind of prescription is likely to ensue from a faulty diagnosis?

Certainly, if the country faces the kind of terrorism as defined in the Crime Committee report, then a responsible government has a duty to specify in some detail, to a patriotic and responsible citizenry, exactly the nature of that threat. Only then should citizens be expected to bear gladly the risks, costs and burdens of a "war". But then, nothing I have heard from the government, read in news accounts, gathered from objective police sources, or witnessed as a trained observer suggests in any unqualified way, shape or form that Jamaica is under threat from either terrorism or its twin "cousin" narco-terrorism—as understood, that is, by specialists in international affairs and in the body of political science literature that has been accumulating since the 1980s.

Taking this position in a *Gleaner*-invited article (Headley 2002; see also Chapter 1), earned me the ire of a few readers. So I welcome the opportunity to elaborate. In doing so, I shall borrow heavily from an academic paper by a colleague criminologist, James Inciardi (1988), of the University of Delaware. The discussion will be in three parts. I will focus in this chapter on key definitional aspects of terrorism. I will then give, in the next chapter, an historical perspective of the phenomenon of narco-terrorism. In the chapter following that, I will argue that neither terrorism nor narco-terrorism, as defined and understood analytically, fits the Jamaican situation.

Terrorism Broadly Defined

In the broadest sense of the term, terrorism is the use of violence for political ends. Terrorism at various times has thus included the acts of indiscriminate aggression that seem to be a by-product of all forms of war. But also thrown into the mix would be the violent repression on the part of governments to quell opposition to its own fractious rules, as Zimbabwe's President Robert Mugabe did in the months leading up to his country's presidential election in early March 2002. Also included are acts of protest of all types when violence is involved. And perhaps most conspicuously are the coordinated activities of revolutionary groups organized to bring about political change, such as those of the Irish Republican Army, Italy's Red Brigades, and the many Middle Eastern groups, like the Palestinian's Hamas and Osama bin Laden's Al Quaeda, operating under the umbrella of Islamic Jihad.

This certainly suggests that what has been called "terrorism" is not a uniquely lonely form of political activity. "Rather, it exists on a continuum from aspects of conventional warfare, through assassination, guerrilla warfare and insurgency (i.e., aggression by small military units for the purpose of establishing liberated zones in which an alternative gov-

> **Terrorism is best defined as the systematic use or threat of extreme violence directed against symbolic victims.**

ernment can be established), sabotage, state repression, persecution, and torture." (Inciardi 1988, p. 7) But despite these differences in perspective, there are a few points on which virtually all terrorism specialists agree:

- Terrorism is almost exclusively a political weapon
- Terrorism is almost always grounded in ideological

18

(not narrow partisan) politics

- Terrorism is a technique of psychological warfare, accomplished primarily through violence directed at innocent, civilian victims
- The victims of terrorist violence are not necessarily the primary targets
- The effects of relatively small amounts of violence tend to be disproportionate to the number of people terrorized, or, to cite an ancient Chinese proverb, "Kill one, frighten ten thousand". (Ibid)

There are other points on which observers of terrorism agree. Terrorists are not simply vandals or ordinary criminals. They always have a political purpose. What they do is done in the name of "justice", although their conception of "justice" often is wildly at odds with that of the rest of the world: liberating Puerto Rico from the terrible Americans, freeing animals from the clutches of mad scientists, or killing abortion doctors "to save innocent life".

From the 'Assassins' of 11th Century Islam to the April 19 ("M-19") guerrillas of Columbia or the Islamic Jihad of the Middle East, there is always a cause to destroy or to kill for. Moreover, the cause need not involve an immediate wrong. It might be revenge for something generations old, as when Armenians murdered Turkish diplomats in the 1980s, because the Turkish (or Ottoman) Empire exterminated thousands of Armenians a long time ago. Or in the 1990s, when Serb nationals in Kosovo slaughtered thousands of ethnic Albanians, because of an historic grievance going all the way back to 1389. None of the original killers need still be alive. Some feuds survive in the blood. Irish Catholics are still revenging themselves on Oliver Cromwell.

Keeping these general guidelines in mind, terrorism is likely best defined as 'the systematic use or threat of extreme violence directed against symbolic victims, typically performed for psychological rather than material effects, for the purpose of coercing individuals, groups, communities, or governments into making political or tactical concessions.' And it is within the context of this definition of terrorism that narco-terrorism might be most appropriately examined.

Narco-Terrorism

The term 'narco-terrorism' was reportedly invented by former Peruvian President Fernando Belaunde to describe the situation developing in his country in the early 1980s. Narco-terrorism suggests an unholy alliance between drugs and terrorism; or, at the very least, a link between drug trafficking and the activities of terrorist groups. While terrorism is a *political* concept, narco-terrorism is an *economic* concept.

Drugs and terrorism got linked in two significant ways. The first was that, for the sake of intimidation and deterrence, some drug trafficking groups were known to use terrorist-*like* activities. A drug don flies up to Miami from Kingston and later that day around the family dinner table he kills, in full view of others, one after the other, half-a-dozen of his lieutenants. Or, more recently, a deep-sea diver working for the Jamaican customs authority is murdered on a lonely country road on his way to work; investigating authorities suspect drug assassins killed him. Activities like these are what the Jamaican government and some in the local news media refer to as 'narco-terrorism', albeit that the violent activities have no connection with what is understood in the literature as terrorism.

The second and altogether more correct link is the involvement in drug trafficking by insurgent groups for the purpose of financing their revolutionary or insurrectionary ventures. Trafficking in narcotics coming to serve, under such circumstances—either through proxies or direct engagement by the insurrectionists themselves—a strictly economic function: that is, for example, to purchase ordnance to blow up a bridge or government building such as a courthouse, or weapons to launch a surprise attack on a military target, say a compound or barracks.

In narco-terrorism, in other words, the guns are the objective and trafficking in narcotics (from growth and manufacture to distribution and sales) is the means. A country does not have a narco-terrorism problem when the trafficking, or control of the trafficking, is the end and the guns merely the means.

3

*Nasty bedfellows*ƒ

Properly understood, narco-terrorism refers to an unholy alliance between drugs and terrorist groups. The term applies, therefore, only to situations of direct or indirect involvement in drug trafficking by insurgent or revolutionary groups for the purpose of financing their 'revolutionary' ventures. By that definition, narco-terrorism is the economic arm to a political project.

The misconception comes when we describe as 'narco-terrorist' the purely *criminal* behaviour of individuals involved in illegal drug trafficking, such as the trademark terrorist-like killings committed by Columbian and Jamaican drug rings. Theirs is a style of murder that leaves no witnesses. However brutal and horrifying killings of this type are, though, devoid of any larger ideological or political content, they are still nothing more than the dirty, horrible work of what are essentially criminal gangs.

ƒ Revised and reprinted with permission, *The Gleaner* (February 17, 2002)

Drug Trafficking and Insurgency

Traditional criminal organizations, several of them with periph-
eral ties in Jamaica, have for decades dominated the international
heroin and cocaine drug trades. But
since the 1980s a number of other
agencies—namely insurgent and/or
revolutionary groups—have,
through various drug-related activi-

> **Terrorist groups got involved in narcotics trafficking for one simple reason: the enormous profits of the drug business**

ties, successfully cut in on the traditional criminal organizations' narcotics turf. These activities, all undertaken for economic purposes, have included:

- Extortion of money from low-level narcotics produc-
  ers (such as peasants who grow opium poppies or coca
  leaves)
- Providing protection to refining and trafficking organizations
- Direct involvement in illegal drug production and distribution, and
- Outright control over drug-producing regions.

It is in these activities that the most direct links between
drugs and terrorism exist. Moreover, it is from these insurgent linkages that narco-terrorism got its name. The insurgent or terrorist groups got involved in narcotics trafficking
for one simple reason: the enormous profits of the drug business.

Other than those terrorist groups whose activities have
been supported by a few rich Arab-oil states, or rich Arabs

like Osama bin Laden, almost all rural insurgents, urban terrorists and liberation movements depended in the past on inexpedient means to fund and sustain their operations: on things like bank robberies, ransom kidnapping, industrial thefts, and donations of money and food. But no bank robbery or kidnapping could compare with the quick infusions of cash generated by illegal drugs, particularly cocaine.

Notably important to the emergence of narco-terrorism has been the tendency for *both* insurgency and drug production to be co-located. Both have existed side by side for some time now in the "Golden Triangle" (Burma, Laos and Thailand), the "Golden Crescent" (Iran, Afghanistan and Pakistan), and the Andes Mountains (Columbia, Bolivia, Peru and Ecuador). This co-location, furthermore, has tended to be concentrated in rural sections of so-called "liberated zones," where government control is weak and unable to effectively manage the activities of either the terrorists or the traffickers.

A glance at narco-terrorism as it emerged in South America is instructive. We'll look briefly at the history and purposes of three narco-terrorist organizations—the FARC, the M-19, and Sendero Luminoso. In the piece that follows, I'll try to unravel what implications flow therefrom for Jamaica. Here, as in the previous chapter, I am leaning heavily on the work of James Inciardi (1988).

The FARC

FARC, the Armed Revolutionary Forces of Columbia, though slimmed down since its glory days of the 1970s and

1980s, is a pro-Marxist revolutionary group which at one time numbered as many as 7,000 members and supporters divided into several dozen guerrilla fronts (see Box 3). Half of the movement's present structure operates in the regions of Columbia's marijuana and cocaine industries. With its formation in 1966 as an armed branch of the pro-Soviet Communist Party, FARC's aim was establishment of a "people's Government."

The Columbian regime, FARC argued, reflected the interests of North American imperialists. To change the political arrangements, FARC adopted guerrilla attacks on the nerve centres of the country. In its early years, FARC had little impact on the Columbian political scene, having limited its activities to symbolic occupation of some remote rural villages. In the mid-1970s, however, FARC went into the ransom kidnapping business. As its income grew, so too did its ambitions.

FARC's entry into the drug trade came in the early 1980s. With payments received in the form of cash or armaments, its narco-terrorism has focussed on four areas:

- Regular collection of protection money from marijuana and coca growers in its operating territories
- Overseeing drug trafficking in certain areas, with collections based on specific quotas
- Providing major Medellin traffickers (the Carlos Ledhers and the Escobars) with guaranteed access to clandestine airfields, and
- Direct involvement in coca growing and refining.

Movimiento 19 de April (M-19)

Columbia's M-19 is another Marxist-inspired insurgent-terrorist group that, though also weakened as a fighting force, after sustained American-backed counter-attacks, was well-known all over South America in the 1980s and early 1990s. Its origins are in the National Popular Alliance (NPA), a minor political party that had been successful enough in the 1960s to be represented in the Columbian Parliament.

In the disputed Presidential election of April 19, 1970, however, the NPA suffered serious losses. To the more extreme in the party the only solution appeared to be armed struggle to achieve its political ends. Originally named after the date of the disputed election, the M-19 (Movimiento 19 de April or 19th of April Movement) officially announced its birth in 1974 by raiding the Simon Bolivar museum outside Bogotá, making off with the sword and spurs of the man who is revered as "the Liberator" of Latin America.

"After its rather theatrical entrance to the world of insurgent-guerrilla movements, the M-19 followed the normal terrorist course of bank robberies, raids on military armouries, kidnappings and killings. Yet it has always had a touch of flamboyance about its activities, giving it considerable publicity." (Inciardi 1988, p. 16) In 1979, the M-19 tunnelled into a Bogotá arsenal to steal armaments; in 1980 it kidnapped all of the guests, including an American Ambassador, attending a cocktail party at the Dominican Republic Embassy in Bogotá; and in 1981 it kidnapped and executed a missionary from the United States.

Originally an urban guerrilla group, the M-19's shift to rural insurgency occurred during the early 1980s. Its involvement in narco-terrorism came shortly thereafter, with activities similar to those of the FARC. In September 1985, M-19 guerrillas seized Columbia's Palace of Justice and murdered 11 Supreme Court justices. M-19 operatives would go on in succeeding years to add trafficking in cocaine to its insurgent activities, profits from which would enable them to equip some 10,000 new rebels.

What the group lacked, however, were sufficient personnel to train these new recruits. Not to worry: they used drug monies to recruit experienced mercenaries from the Miami area to serve as trainers for M-19's future skirmishes with the Columbian military. Recruited "sicarios" (or gunmen) by major drug traffickers were trained in M-19 camps. After assassinating their targets (typically those judges, prosecutors, and journalists who dared to oppose the drug cartel barons), the sicarios would be sent back to Miami, essentially to "cool out," before embarking on their next assignment.

In later years, the M-19 Movement would splinter into different political and rebel factions. One splinter, the National Liberation Army (ELN), fiercely continues the terrorist cause.

Sendero Luminoso

Sendero Luminoso, or Shining Path, emerged from a tangled web of Peruvian Maoist politics in 1970. The movement suffered its greatest setback under the Alberto Fujimori regime, especially with the capture of its spiritual leader, Abimael Guzman. But it is still very much alive and kicking.

Noting the striking class differences in his society, Guzman had concluded that as Peru approached the 21st century, it was still a semi-feudal and semi-colonial society. Moreover, the Government embodied a fascist structure masquerading as a democracy. Only by making revolutionaries out of Peruvian peasants could social reform be realized, Guzman contended.

"Sendero Luminoso first came to widespread public attention after a full decade of dogmatic self-examination and rigorously selective recruitment. The violence against the State began in July 1980, and by the end of the year some 240 incidents had been recorded, including the destruction of local tax records, bombings of Government offices and sabotage of electricity pylons." (Inciardi 1988, p. 19) By 1981, the rate of incidents increased and had expanded to such activities as the raiding of banks, mines, and police posts. Kidnapping was added the following year. Sendero's most spectacular action took place early in 1982, when 159 guerrillas attacked the Ayacucho jail and set some 300 prisoners free.

In 1987, direct evidence of a Sendero Luminoso/cocaine link came to light; its most lucrative arrangement being extortion of protection money from coca growers and cocaine traffickers. The practice continues today. In areas controlled by the rebel group, growers are expected to turn over a share of their profits, and traffickers are charged upwards of 5,000 U. S. dollars in "departure fees" for each planeload of coca paste shipped out of the area. Sendero has repeatedly opposed coca eradication projects, not only to protect its stake in drug profiteering, but also for the sake of retaining local peasant support.

I have tried to sketch here the broad contours of the three major groups that have literally defined the term "narco-terrorism," paying special attention to each group's history and purpose. My objective is to raise for critical discussion the question: What in any of what has been described resembles, or is conceivably connected to, Jamaican drug trafficking?

Box 3

Guerrilla Offensive Rocks Columbia as New President Promises Peace

Mario Murillo

Bogotá—Conservative Party leader Andres Pastrana was sworn in on August 7 as Columbia's thirty-seventh President amidst rising expectations that he will bring an end to the country's 40-year civil war. Ending the Liberal Party's 12-year hold on the nation's highest office, Pastrana pledged to fight government corruption through political reform and to implement a structural-adjustment program to "put Columbia's economic house in order." Most important, the new President said he would personally take a leading role in eventual peace negotiations with the country's two largest guerrilla organizations, the Revolutionary Armed Force of Columbia (FARC) and the National Liberation Army (ELN).

Pastrana outlined a number of steps aimed at achieving peace and national reconciliation. Among the new initiatives was the creation of a National Fund for Peace to meet the immense costs of carrying out comprehensive peace negotiations. The President claimed that the fund would be paid for by resources freed up by the government's austerity program, support from the international community, and a special "peace tax," which would have to be approved by the Columbian Congress. The tax would also require a financial commitment from the country's business elite to a settlement of the conflict. It remains to be seen whether the country's business community will agree to underwrite the cost of peace and whether neo-liberal austerity can, in the long run, contribute to pacification of the country.

While Pastrana's announcements were received with optimism, his "program for peace" was overshadowed by a massive guerrilla offensive in 14 of the country's 31 departments in the days leading up to the transfer of power. The offensive resulted in at least 69 casualties for the army and the National Police. In what was seen as the latest and perhaps most humiliating defeat in recent months, over 100 soldiers and anti-narcotics police were captured by the FARC, raising the total number of state security personnel currently being held by the guerrillas to 220.

The heaviest guerrilla attack occurred in the southeastern municipality of Miraflores in the department of Guaviare—the heart of Columbia's coca-growing region. In recent years, Miraflores has been the focus of a U.S.-backed coca-eradication campaign. As a guerrilla stronghold, this municipality has seen a dramatic increase in paramilitary violence against the civilian population. In the August 3 offensive, some 300 FARC combatants ambushed a joint army-police anti-narcotics base, killing 30 soldiers and police officers and completely destroying the base.

. . . Pastrana did not allow the offensive to derail his plan to demilitarize five municipalities in the southern departments of Meta and Caqueta in order to lay the groundwork for an eventual dialogue with the FARC.

The move was seen as a victory for the guerrillas, who have been demanding the demilitarization of this vast territory for over 18 months as a prerequisite for the peace talks. The President said that the military withdrawal from the region would take place within 90 days, during which the two sides would establish a framework for negotiations. Pastrana warned the guerrillas that the demilitarization should not be taken as a cover to engage in what he called their business dealings with drug traffickers. . .

Excerpted and reprinted with permission, **NACLA: Report on the Americas** *Volume XXXII (No. 2, September/October), 1998, pp. 1-2*

4

'Every posse get flat'*f*

"It's a cold Saturday night in January. A group of revellers, a microcosm of the Jamaican working class, which had to go abroad in order to find work, are celebrating in typical yard style the end of the working week. They are doing so in one of the new reggae hot spots that have been springing up like wild orchids amid the interstices of the 'concrete jungles' of Chicago's North Side. Between the live, on stage performances of a local reggae band, the party people are jamming to recorded soca music . . .

"Over by the bar, some of the older men, now properly juiced on Jamaican rum and Red Stripe Beer, are engrossed in a rambling discussion on Jamaican politics. Talk, like the liquor, is cheap.

"A group of younger men dressed in the latest styles and fashion of their hip-hop generation saunters in from off the bustling sidewalk. A couple of them begin a friendly banter

---

f Revised and reprinted with permission, *The Gleaner* (February 24, 2002)

over the price of admission with the woman cloistered behind the bulletproof Plexiglas enclosure at the entranceway.
They pay it and then enter the hall with a slow, deliberate gait
. . . Across the dance floor heads, shoulders, arms, and waists
are gyrating in a steady, rhythmic, pulsating roll. In striking
contrast to the shivering, sub-zero temperature outside, the
room is hot, steamy. *Dis a seshaan, mahn!*

Bagfuls of cocaine seized by Jamaica Defence Force in Belmont, Westmoreland, in early 2002

"Then sometime between midnight and the wee hours of
the breaking new day, about the time that local ordinances
require that all liquor sales cease, the air is pierced by the
deafening sound of what to the untrained ear seems like an
earth-shattering distortion coming from one of the giant

speakers which had been pumping out steady streams of thou-sand-odd-watt music all night long. But when the noise re-peats itself in quick, rapid-fire bursts, the music for the moment uninterrupted, the revellers realize that this is no stereophonic distortion: this is the sound of gunfire. The laughter and the gaiety that only a few moments before had filled the room is replaced by the shrieks of frightened men and women, punctured by cries of 'Lawd Jesus Chris!'

"Everyone runs for cover. The tune 'Every Posse Get Flat' now suddenly takes on the literal, deadly meaning for which it must have been intended. The bartender cowers beneath the bar. One diminutive man dives into a freestanding trashcan. The sound man, who only hours before had exercised extreme care in setting up his expensive gadgetry, now uses those same gadgets to barricade himself. The carnival comes to an abrupt stop.

"From their flattened positions and with both hands pressed against the backs of their heads, the petrified patrons begin cautiously, slowly, to peer into the centre of the darkened room as they try to comprehend what had 'hit' them. Standing there are two of Jamaica's 'children of Sisyphus': a couple of uprooted, unrighteous toughs dressed in tams and designer-labelled warm-up outfits, their heavily tinted sunglasses menacingly set against the din and smoke coming from hastily discarded cigarettes. Around their necks hang half of Africa's gold reserve. Their itchy fingers are nervously coiled around the trigger mechanisms of two of civilisation's most awesome solutions for the Malthusian problem of too many people. Using converted submachine guns, the youths had just mowed down, at point-blank range, two male revellers, whose chests are torn apart by rounds of hollow point bullets. Blood oozes from their riddled, dying bodies like water from a broken standpipe. The scene is straight out of Dodge.

"The gunmen, in typical cowboy style, had busted their way into the hall. They had a dispute to 'settle' with their victims. That dispute, over either drug turf or drug money, was now settled in a decisive, final way. Their mission of waste, death, and destruction accomplished, the marauders, still clutching the smoking instruments of death with firm, sinewy hands, stealthily back away from the carnage and out through the swinging doors. They speed off into the winter night in a shiny, vanity-license-plated silver BMW." (Excerpted from Headley 1996, pp. 1-2)

A Type of Crime

I retell the above story because in its unfolding are the central elements of what fundamentally characterize the kind or type of crime from which the Jamaican government's crime proposals (Box 2), under National Security Minister Dr. Peter Phillips, seek to give the Jamaican people relief. Within the same timeframe of that Chicago incident—in the late 1980s—the American authorities recorded an additional 1400 such killings. That is, brutal, horrific slayings, committed by Jamaican gang enforcers (either living in or passing through the United States) of others with whom they had a dispute over drug turf or drug money. Vigorous engagement of all the forces at its command against that kind of crime is what the Jamaican government has embarked upon. It's doing so under the banner of a "war against terrorism," specifically against "narco-terrorism."

But hardly does unequivocal evidence exist that would support a correct terrorist assessment of the Jamaican situation, certainly not in the immense body of intelligence information that international law enforcement has collected over the years on drug-related activities of Jamaican gangs, at home and abroad. Close examination of typical Jamaican involvement in the illegal drug trade reveals certain standard items, none of which bears tangible resemblance to what constitutes terrorism, or narco-terrorism.

The items are:

- The arena of operation is exclusively in trafficking, as both wholesalers and distributors; doing so in lucrative direct sales of cocaine and cocaine derivatives in places like Brooklyn, and in appropriating as payment layers of transhipped powdered cocaine coming through Jamaica on its way to the U. S. and Great Britain. Unlike Columbia and Peru's *narco-trafficantes*, Jamaica's drug gangs, and their business-political patrons, have zero interest in owning or controlling "politically liberated" zones. More important to them is gaining access to things like shipping containers and on-shore warehouses, and in either "owning" or "renting" an assortment of overseas couriers and transporters—so-called "mules".
- The business of narcotics' trafficking among Jamaican entities is unencumbered by extraneous politically

organized forces. There are no interlocking director-
ships or super-ordinate terrorist echelons dictating to
or extorting from the Jamaican posses, as the FARC
and M-19 outfits have for years been doing to the
Columbian cartels. In the absence of any form of organized terrorist intrusion, there is, therefore, in Jamaican drug trafficking, no hint of a larger political or
ideological intent, such as overthrowing the Government or bringing down any of its institutions. Illegal
gain is the only game, and moving and selling drugs
the only agenda. The objective, straight up, is to own,
or at least be able to control, as much as possible aspects of the trade.

- Present political arrangements are just fine, particularly since a high level of well-nurtured cosiness exists
between local drug "kingpins" (such as there are), select senior political operatives, and agents of the state,
particularly within the top tiers of the security forces.
These all make for non-antagonistic working relationships—this notwithstanding the gangs from time to
time coming under surprise, rear guard police liqui-
dating missions.

Within Jamaican drug gangs there is, indeed, reflexive
readiness to resort to a type of violence that is undeniably
"terrorist-like." But that extreme mode of conduct is still not
terrorism. Unlike the violence of known terrorist groups like
the Irish Republic Army or Hamas' suicide bombers, whose
violence more often than not is "wasted" on things like blow-
ing up buses filled with schoolchildren, merely to send a mes-

sage or make a point, the violence that is characteristic of Jamaican drug gangs is ruthlessly utilitarian, expedient; it "takes care of business" in the narrow *criminal* sense. It represents a mindset, and an approach, that for generations gestated in the belly of the Jamaican beast.

Police, Super Cop, & Peacemaking

5

Why aren't we all more cooperative with the police?

Why is the Jamaican police unable to follow through with successful arrests and prosecution of known criminals and gunmen? It's a pressing question that the Jamaican public in its perpetual angst over crime and violence keeps asking.

The chief reason for this non-cooperation, a commonly held thesis posits, is a prevailing "code of ethics" among thieves and criminals, and inside ghetto communities, that views with extreme disfavour any complicity with outsiders, especially with the police. Law enforcement is thus unable to make airtight cases against street level drug dons, because witnesses view as the greater evil—greater indeed than the dons' crimes—the "evil" of cooperating with the authorities.

Police officials say they are flabbergasted at the phenomenon. Generous offers and guarantees of protection have not resulted in any mad rush of witnesses into the stationhouse.

I will leave aside for purpose of this discussion the truth that global law enforcement nowadays relies less on eyewitness or informer accounts for successful criminal prosecutions. More convincing for putting away villains, sometimes for life, are scientific methodologies for gathering and analysing physical and other circumstantial evidence, than in relying on oft-times unreliable memories and impaired visions of eyewitnesses. (Osama bin Laden's Al Quaeda forces are being obliterated by American-led forces without a single person having laid eyes on any of them boarding an American airplane on the morning of September 11, 2001.)

We are still left to ponder, though, why the failure to communicate between residents often disproportionately affected by crime—especially violent crime—and the police. Explanations of police excessive use of deadly force and their "terrorist" tactics, particularly as regards the poor, are helpful—more so than do police attempts to explain away the problem as resulting from a "culture of silence" among ghetto people. But these only get to one side of the story, because neither has the Jamaican public at large shown excessive willingness to embrace their police force. That other side the nation will have to face forthrightly if its people are to arrive at a true consensus on crime. Two factors, I suggest, have worked against any meaningful cooperative front:

I.   The social reality of crime in Jamaica—its occurrence as well as formal and informal reactions to it—is constrained by disparate or differently affected interests.

II. The police institution, which inherently reflects one element of a fundamental divide in the society, is yet to be part of a greater "us."

Pockets of Affected Interest

The crimes that most worry the Jamaican populace affect them in different and grossly disproportionate ways. We encounter serious, violent crime depending on where we are in the society, both in terms of physical location and within the social structure. If we live in the Kingston Metropolitan Area (which accounts for more than 60 percent of all serious crime), we would normally encounter and then talk about crime in ways that depend on whether we:

- Are from the up-town professional middle or upper social classes
- Represent elite private sector business interests
- Are apparatchiks within one of the two rival political party organizations
- Are poor ghetto residents residing in areas riddled with crime.

If we are from the professional middle or upper social classes, the everyday crimes that affect us are not in any way related to Wild West-type gunfire. The crimes we most frequently encounter are more like nuisance crimes. Sure, we have suffered from the occasional gardener gone berserk. Neighbours some of us knew—or knew of—have a time or two ended up as victims of a seemingly random street-type killing. A few hoodlums have found ingenious and sometimes frightening ways to relieve several young people in (or visiting) the community of their Toyotas. And ever so often a "Most Wanted" gunman and remnants of his crew take sanctuary (while fleeing from the police) among his kinfolk nestled in one of our pocket or fringe squatter settlements.

But mostly our everyday crime concerns have more to do with monitoring the mango tree in the yard for barefaced thieves, and remembering to take in clothes not quite dry off the clothesline. If we were to truthfully say what irks us most, it would be the crass coarseness in the society and the daredevil idiots who speed up and down our quiet neighbourhood streets. As long as the police and hired security keep violent crime in downtown Kingston, and prevent people from blocking Mountain View Road when we need to get to the Norman Manley airport in a hurry, crime is not really for us a personal, terribly big deal.

The police we are otherwise aware of, our experience with them pretty much confined to dinner-table tales about our speed-trap and spot check run-ins with them—though we do feel reassured when they lead long motorised cavalcades through our neighbourhoods.

If we are from the commercial and business elite, no getting away from it, crime—certainly images of violent crime—hurts our bottom line, especially our tourist industry. Serious violent crime is not something we had before given much thought to, until two of our people were viciously murdered back in the 1970s. But we weren't really concerned throughout the 1960s, when we were doing quite well—though, so we have been made to understand, substantial numbers of people were amassing into what would become gigantic urban slums. Hence, we were rather surprised, "shocked," at living conditions back in the summer of 2001, when Member of Parliament Edward Seaga took us on a tour of his West Kingston constituency—after violence there threatened to bring the whole house down (Chapter 7). Can you believe it?

The police, as far as we are concerned, simply need to do what has to be done. They need to get a hold of this thing, to manage crime. Bring it under control. It matters little to us how they do it. Get overseas help. Ask the university business school people to come up with a plan.

If we are functionaries for one of the two leading political party organizations, crime, including violent crime, is not exactly for us a clear-cut, easily definable, unambiguous matter. "What's a few broken bones in the birth of the nation?" a People's National Party founding father, Wills O. Issacs, asked in all earnestness at the dawn of the new Jamaica (in the 1940s). He was not, of course, talking about how to prepare beef soup. He was, instead, giving validation to a method for gaining and holding on to power—turf warfare—which would be the touchstone of urban political struggle for generations to come. Many youthful martyrs would be sacrificed in that struggle. Their side attacks, and ours have to defend. The best defence is a solid offence.

For these violent political tug-of-wars, the police have learned that it is essential for them to understand from which side their bread gets buttered. More times than not, they are tacitly instructed to "stand by."

Then, finally, if we are from the Kingston shantytowns,

our trauma is for real. Our mothers have cried many rivers, and never for us "a moment that the moans don't come double." A crust of bread and a street corner to sleep on, our short, little existence lived as fodder for deadly plans and schemes we do not always understand—before it is ended face down on the hot asphalt. And that is life.

Back in 1965 the Reverend W. A. Blake described our situation this way: "Many persons live in cardboard huts which could collapse in the wet weather . . . Close the Coronation Market and Back O' Wall would be rapidly depopulated—the people there ate chiefly on Thursday, Friday and Saturday. Relatives from the country visiting the market often brought food on those days. . . The effect on family life would be illustrated by the case of a girl whose mother told her at the age of ten that she could no longer feed her; the girl took to scuffling for herself, and was half-starved, became a prostitute, now at eighteen has a baby whose father is in prison." (Quoted in Headley 1982)

In September 2001, a Kingston youngster, Traudl Benson-Bray, penned this way, in a *Gleaner*-sponsored school poetry competition, deteriorating developments in those same underlying conditions described 36 years earlier by Blake:

> *Gentle Jesus meek and mild*
>
> *Gunshot down here really wild*
>
> *So I will soon be there with Thee*
>
> *Mom won't have to pay school fee.*
>
> (Quoted with permission)

You would think that, given our in-and-out-of-foxhole situation, our natural ally, and the people to whom we would run when things steamed up, or when the pressure dropped, would be the police. Not at all! The police only seem to add to our distress—least of which is their bad sociology of us.

Which leads to the second major item in this discussion.

Police Not on Our Side

Esteemed University of the West Indies, Mona, colleague, Anthony Harriott, has already pointed out in his well-received book, *Police and Crime Control in Jamaica* (2000), that in its present organization, mode of operation, mindset and attitudes, today's Jamaica Constabulary Force (JCF) is not strikingly different from its original creation back in 1865. The JCF, as established then (at the behest of the plantocracy and in the wake of the Morant Bay Rebellion) was a paramilitary force trained and equipped to put down the insurrectionary movements of the country's black masses.

An outside agency, the Police Executive Research Forum, brought here by the American Chamber of Commerce (whose visit the JCF endorsed) to look at the way the JCF operates, arrived at pretty much the same conclusion as Harriott: the JCF's method of policing, notably its penchant for squads, serves little else but to terrorize (my word) the population, an approach that is bound to fail.

The easiest analogy is what happened with the American effort in Vietnam. Undoubtedly large numbers of Vietnamese, specifically in the South, never cared much for the communist "criminals" who had infiltrated their midst in the 1950s and early 1960s. Initial, well-intentioned U. S. forces sought only to support those "decent" (shall we say law-abiding?) communities wanting to rid their land of the godforsaken communists. Later, when the U. S. method of support manifested itself in terms of indiscriminate carpet bombings and slash-and-burn warfare against whole villages, destroying them in order to "save" them, the only thing that was accomplished was the radicalisation of an entirely affected nation against the very forces that had come to rescue it. After ten years of dismal failure, the Americans ignominiously hightailed it out of Vietnam, suffering its only military defeat.

The ruling myth within Jamaican law enforcement is that, within the country's midst, is a discrete, well-defined enemy army of criminal combatants, against whom "we" have no choice but to wage all out war. This enemy army, as observed in the violent West Kingston events of July 7-10 (Chapter 7), according to police and army testimony, can successfully penetrate and submerge itself within the civilian population of women and children, which then gives it shelter and material support. The only way we can go after this "army," and thereby rid the society of crime, is to launch a full-scale frontal assault on it; flush it out, bring it "into the open" where we can "deal" with it, to quote supreme crime management commander, Senior Superintendent Reneto Adams (following chapter). Carpet-bomb its daylights, wherever and with whomever we find it.

The problem with that is, *it's not policing!* It's called rightfully what the nation's current law enforcement and national security regime say it is: war. But it's a war that is unintelligent—and un-winnable.

Man on a mission*f*

Senior Police Superintendent Reneto Adams is the tough cop Prime Minister P. J. Patterson in late 2000 named to head a new police unit, the Crime Management Unit (CMU). The CMU is in effect an anti-crime squad within an existing anti-crime squad. But the reasoning behind its creation was that, in dealing with the country's spiralling violent crime, the CMU would play a more combative, in your face, take-it-to-the-hoodlums type role in a directed frontal assault on particularly street and gang-related crimes.

Horrific, indeed, have been the country's serious crime figures, especially for violent or personal crimes. Of the 1,139 people killed violently in 2001, in this island of two and a half-million inhabitants, more than 60 per cent were at the hands of vengeful gunmen and irate family members, according to the police. Fifty of the dead were children killed in crossfire between fighting inner-city gangs (Statistical Department,

f Revised and reprinted with permission, *Social and Economic Studies* 51 (No 1, March) 2002.

(c) The Gleaner Co. Ltd

Commissioner's Office 2002). And the police admitted their role in at least another 135 extra-judicial slayings. The numbers for all such incidents represent substantial increases over the previous year, when the number of murders for all that year stood at (a not insignificant) 887. This upward trend has placed Jamaica among a select group of "top" three or four nations with the dubious distinction of continuously having in recent years the highest homicide rates in the world.

Added to that, in the early months of 2001, tribal-political warlords, *and* drug lords, successfully brought into the island guns and ammunition in quantities that suggested "the bargain sales" at which they must have been acquired overseas had "only days to end," as Jamaica *Gleaner* reporter Lloyd Williams (2001) shrewdly put it. Moreover, according to Minister of National Security Peter Phillips, the amount of cocaine passing through Jamaica each year generates "a tremendous inflow of resources that could destabilize a small state like Jamaica" (*The Gleaner*, November 23, 2001).

Still, the job Adams has—essentially that of getting both the guns and the criminals off the streets—is one many (though certainly not most) Jamaicans believe he has taken far too seriously. His unit has been responsible for a new spate of police killings, causing several spokespersons for leading local human rights organizations to call for his removal and disbanding of the CMU. Some, notably leading representatives of the group Families Against State Terrorism, have wondered aloud, on nationwide radio talk shows, if Adams may not be taking grotesque pleasure from his monstrous accomplishments, and from the way he has defined his mission. That mission, as they have been saying they understand it—based on Adams' numerous public utterances, especially to the media—is that he wants to bring in more dead than alive elements from the society's presumed dangerous classes.

In March 2001 Adams' unit shot and killed seven mostly teenage boys holed up in a small house in Braeton, in the parish of St. Catherine, a bedroom community to the capital city of Kingston (*The Gleaner*, March 16, 2001). Sixty armed police officers went to the house to serve two arrest-warrants in the early morning hours of March 14. The officers said "men in the house fired on them as they approached," and that they fired back, killing all seven on the spot. "The days of criminals shooting at the police are over," Adams declared triumphantly at the death scene, into television cameras.

Neighbours and other eyewitnesses recalled to news reporters an entirely different series of events, however. They said someone let the police into the house, after which they questioned and beat the young men before executing them. One of the young men was executed outside the house for trying to rally support of his friends who were cornered by the police inside the house. The Council of the Jamaican Bar Association described the killing of the seven young men as "highly suspicious" and involving the possibility of "cold-blooded murder" (*The Gleaner*, March 22, 2001). A Coroner's Court would, in late 2002, render a narrow split decision absolving the police of criminal wrongdoing.

On July 7, four months following the Braeton incident, an operation Adams and his men embarked upon ended with

25 civilians being killed, plus two members of the security forces (Box 4). Adams would admit in public testimony to a Commission of Enquiry looking into that set of events (next chapter), attended by the author, that he knew, "for sure," that in that operation he "personally shot and killed a number of persons [not included in the 25] who were shooting at the police." But the authorities never recovered their bodies because, Adams offered, residents had burned them in mass graves in the vicinity of nearby May Pen Cemetery (author's notes).

Thirty-eight other persons were shot and injured by Adams' forces during that operation, one of them a young girl whose eyes were shot out by a bullet after it penetrated the eight-inch-thick concrete wall of her high-rise apartment building; and another whose leg was shredded by a shell as she lay in her bed. Mass (and mostly political opposition-inspired) demonstrations, stretching as far as the western end of the island, followed the shootings, resulting in at least two more deaths. The combination of events from July 7 to 10—including the sight of dead bodies left rotting on the streets—gave the country a black eye internationally, hurting especially its major foreign exchange earner, tourism, and putting off potential foreign investors, damage from which it had not yet recovered when hit even more devastatingly by the terrorist attacks on the United States on September 11, 2001.

The slain teenage boys in Braeton the police had suspected of murdering a schoolteacher and a policeman. And the killings in West Kingston, Adams would say in open, public testimony, were of individuals who had either shot at the security forces (i.e., police and army), or they were persons caught in a line of fire while giving cover to gunmen shooting at the security forces (author's notes). The security forces had merely "fired back," after coming under attack from bands of gunmen using high-powered weaponry, including AK-47 assault riffles and missiles fired from rocket launchers. His forces were in the area carrying out a lawful search for drugs and guns, Adams would tell the Commission of Enquiry (ibid).

The extreme actions taken by the security forces that July Saturday morning had resulted in calls for Patterson to set up the Commission of Enquiry. The calls came from civil society and more vociferously from the political opposition, led by its leader Edward Seaga, in whose constituency, notably in the vicinity of his Tivoli Gardens stronghold, the killings occurred.

Seaga repeatedly contended on radio talk shows that "no such fire" as Adams claimed was ever directed at the security forces. Rather, he insisted, the government, wanting to hold on to power, but having only a short time to go before having to face an electorate likely to turn them out of office, used raw state power—"200 police and soldiers firing some 22,000 rounds of ammunition," according to Seaga—to unleash terror, as it had done many times before, on a politically disfavoured population.

I attended a number of the Commission's public hearings, at which I took copious notes. Mostly I wanted to learn from primary sources—like Adams—their version of the events in question. I ended up achieving a measure of greater clarity on a number of different aspects relative to Jamaica's crime situation (next chapter).

Between early September 2001 and the end of February 2002, the Commission of Enquiry sat and heard mostly unsuccessfully challenged police and army testimony. This because of procedural rules set up by the Commission under its Chair, Grenadian-born Julius Isaac, a retired Canadian high court jurist whom Patterson recruited for the job. The rules in effect precluded on technical and highly controversial grounds lawyers representing oppositionist interests—namely Seaga, the JLP, and the victim community—from cross-examining witnesses.

And herein lie two prime difficulties with Commissions of Enquiry in Jamaica and elsewhere in the Caribbean: (a) their essential politicisation, and (b) their tendency, in the end, to find no fault with official or state action. Commissions of Enquiry are, according to Chapman (1973), fundamentally bodies "set up by a government to consider a specific problem or problems. [They] work within clearly indicated constraints of time, resources and, in particular, the political environment" (quoted in Jones 1978: 292). Jones (1978: 295) goes further, with particular reference to the naming of Commissioners and work of Commissions of Enquiry in Jamaica. Recruitment of Commissioners "is inherently a political act," he contends. And "those selected as Commissioners are usually willing to operate within existing configurations, [knowing] that if they breach the socio-political and economic values of the normative order, their report might never be made public." Commission of Enquiry reports have served little else but to, at one level, legitimise the status quo; and at another to justify or find blameless questionable state action.[1]

Left dutifully appearing before the Commission of Enquiry into the West Kingston events were the Commission's own attorneys and teams of expensive lawyers, each representing the army, the police, and the governing PNP. A smaller, and certainly lesser paid, number of advocates from the Attorney General's Office and the recently created office of the Public Defender put in less frequent appearances. But not heard from, for reasons still wrapped in intrigue, if not purely on technicality[2], were the people from the poor ghetto communities who came directly under Senior Superintendent Adams' fire.

Flair and Unwavering Belief

The nation that the senior police officer has in his own way been diligently serving has, though, one—and only one— image of him. It's the image, a powerful one, filtered through television lenses, and usually stage-managed by Adams himself. His visage is usually deliberately set against an urban battlefront, from which he presents a helmeted, balaclava-clad, tough-talking man of war. The public hearings of the Commission on October 29 and 30 gave the Jamaican people, however, a rare opportunity to listen to and observe, in a unique setting, their chief crime management strategist.

Adams came across in the hearings as an instantly likeable man. He smiled easily, was polite, and deferential. He exuded graceful charm that could have easily struck one as dissonant with what he does for a living. He was also well dressed. On both days he appeared he sported expensive, finely tailored suits that fitted perfectly his precise, supremely conditioned frame. He looked as if he had just walked off the pages of an *Esquire* magazine—the bow tie he wore on his first day giving a kind of grandiloquent flair to his witticisms and repartee with his interlocutors.

Since Adams is intensely listened to by the country's national security elite, and is more admired than vilified across broad segments of the society, I thought it important to peer beneath his helmeted façade; to get to know what might be his intended purpose, paying special attention to his language (and the structure of that language), and the information and worldview it conveys. I thought it essential, in other words, to "deconstruct" him. He seemed more than happy to expand with me, in conversations back stage to the Commission's formal hearings, on many of his already on-the-record remarks, while adding of course new commentary.

Adams is, first and foremost, passionately committed to, and an unwavering believer in, the righteousness of his particular project. He knows and clearly understands, in his own mind, his special mission here on earth—his unblinking conception of which should give all concerned Jamaicans pause. He says that he does believe in democratic governance and civilian rule of law (personal interview, October 29, 2001). But he is at the same time intolerant of the ambiguity and ofttimes necessary greyness in the formulation and implementation of public policy, and of the general give-and-take that characterizes democratic systems (ibid).

It is not difficult to imagine Adams being completely at home with, working hard and being highly commended by, the *generalisimos* who ruled much of Latin America, with "firm" hands, up through the early years of the 1980s. He abhors particularly the timidity of Caribbean leaders on the matter of dealing with crime. The Jamaican government, and people, "want and expect" him and his unit to reduce crime and violence in the society. Yet, he says, officials in Government and certain, select sectors of civil society get all squeamish when he and his men "go after the criminals." What do they want him to do, he asks: "hug criminals"? (Ibid.)

He sees the Jamaica Constabulary Force (JCF), for which he works, as weak-kneed. And he agrees with critics that it is not as effective as it ought to be. But this he attributes to politicians' and civilian heads' "deliberate plan" (begun in the Michael Manley 1970's era) to remove from the police force its militaristic praxis, ethos, and *esprit de corps*; in effect neutering it (ibid). The nation's other security arm, the Jamaica Defence Force (JDF), does not entirely consist for Adams, though, of brave hearts. He recalled in open session to the Commission of Enquiry that, while coming "under heavy fire" on the streets of West Kingston in the morning hours of July 7, he saw at one time, safely cocooned in his M-150 (a military vehicle), a young platoon commander.

His is a peculiar twist on reggae singer and polemicist Peter Tosh's well-articulated "No justice, no peace." For Adams, who says he has thought long and hard, and "read a lot about these things," war is a necessary precursor to any sort of sustainable peace (personal interview, October 29, 2001). "History has shown," he argues, without being specific, "that before there is peace, there is a war" (ibid). Only after a war, in which all opposing enemy forces have been taken out—or at least physically neutralized and rendered harmless—can there be sustained peace (ibid).

Jamaica will "never ever, once and for all," root out its serious violent crime problem, Adams insists, until the Jamaican people accept what it is they are up against (ibid). Once they get to that place of full and resigned understanding, they cannot then but accept the inevitable "solution." (Personal interview, October 29, 2001) What the country is up against, Adams insists, is a ruthless bunch of diehard criminals with whom there is "no room for dialogue." They are people against whom war, with its unrelenting logic of waste, death, and destruction, is the only answer.

The Senior Police Superintendent did not shrink, either in my conversation with him or in his public testimony to the Commission of Enquiry, from referring to his approach to dealing with crime in Jamaica as the "final solution." I wondered, but did not ask, if he was fully aware of "final solution" precedents in recent African and European history, which he would likely be following.

Still, startlingly, Adams said he's a believer in community policing. I gathered from our conversation, though, that his idea of community policing was rather convoluted and perhaps intentionally tautological. Community policing means having "safe communities," he said; communities where residents can go about their business and move freely, only because practitioners of "tough" conventional policing, like him, have performed well their task. When I described to him models of community policing that are working successfully (in cities in the United States and Canada), he said it would be impossible in Jamaica, not with Jamaica's mostly unedu- cated inner-city residents. Besides, he conjectured, commu- nity policing is "soft policing" that, within the social confines and precarious ecological logistics of Kingston's urban ghet- tos, would be an open invitation for gunmen and narcotics traffickers to "pick off" policemen (personal interview, Octo- ber 29, 2001).

Problem of Modernity

Chief police attorney, the eminently respected Queen's Council, Ian Ramsay (who defended the plotters of the 1983 Grenadian "counterrevolution"), unwittingly provided an op- portunity to delve into yet another angle to Adams' worldview. During Adams' time on the stand before the Commission, Ramsay prodded him for his views on the sweeping social and cultural changes taking place, and *have taken place*, in Jamaica.

Those views led me to the conclusion that, perhaps what really drives Adams after all, is a grand fundamentalist de- sign: a design to not only rescue or "take back" *his* country, but also to return it to the pristine state he once knew.

In the Jamaica they grew up in (between say the late 1940s and early 1960s), bantered Ramsay and Adams, to the obvi- ous annoyance of Commission Chair Julius Isaac, commu- nities worked harmoniously and peacefully together. And they often did so across boundaries—physical and also political, racial, and social. Proper and accessible role models were "local schoolteachers and village elders, like the parson and village barber"—not citified youths with loads of money, fancy automobiles, and their nine-millimetres. "The barefoot boy from down the road," in his rural Jamaica, Adams offered, could feel free to walk onto the veranda of the house of his better-off neighbour and "sit down and reason with him," without rancour or unduly constructed class barrier between them. It was all so simple then. If only we could get back to those "good old days."

The lament is classic fundamentalist retrospection. It is selective retrieval, going back in thought and imagination to that perfect moment, a moment in history when a particular book, leader, and social order were perfect. "It's all a very particular interpretation, and the fundamentalist convinces us that it's always been there," observes Martin E. Marty (in Scott 2001: 19), an American scholar, of what he terms "fundamentalism projects."

The implications are disturbing. There was for Adams that "perfect" Jamaican moment—perhaps an entire "perfect era." It is the people who have experimented with modernity and instilled corrupt values of materialism and worship of false gods like money (perhaps also of tall buildings) who have gotten us into the mess we're in. He is insistent that the country needs to get back to "basics," to get back to historical-cultural fundamentals.

When asked by Commission Chair Julius Isaac why 27 people had to die so violently, and if it could have been avoided, Adams' typically expansive response was: "It is the duty of government . . . and every government over the last twenty to thirty years has failed. If persons were not motivated, if these criminals were not motivated by other elements in the society, if they were properly socialised along lines of civility and decency, we could have avoided that also." (Author's notes)

Commissioner of Police Francis Forbes has, subsequent to the violent West Kingston events, ordered a review of Adams' Crime Management Unit. The JLP has gone farther. Its leaders have been campaigning on the promise that, in the next general election (scheduled to be called no later than early 2003), should it be elected to run the country, among its first order of business will be to remove Adams from front-line police duty and to disband his notorious anti-crime unit. But, should either Forbes or the JLP move hastily against Adams, they will have to reckon with a Jamaican public that is as fearful of, as it is riled-up over, the issue of violent crime.

Not so surprisingly, that public overwhelmingly approves of Adams and the way it understands him to be fulfilling his crime-fighting mission. In late November 2001, a national survey of more than 1200 Jamaicans, conducted by the reputable Stone Organization, reported that six of every 10 Jamaicans wanted Adams to remain at his post. Fully 60 per cent said he should not be removed, "against 26 per cent who wanted him to go" (*Jamaica Observer 2001*). Not known is what, if any, impact careful reflection on the full weight of Adams' thinking and philosophical leanings would have had on those findings.

Box 4

Violence subsides in Jamaica, but wounds still fester

David Gonzalez

Kingston, Jamaica, July 11—The violence in which 21 civilians have died in the West Kingston slums since the weekend has subsided. The corpses that had been festering in the streets have been removed.

But the bullet hole that cut through apartment walls, the sandbags in the windows of an improvised military command post and the squads of soldiers with their rifles remain as reminders that the country has been shaken by its deadliest clashes in decades.

The violence erupted on Saturday, when the police entered the Tivoli Gardens neighborhood looking for weapons in an effort to stop a war between politically connected gangs that had been simmering for two months. The police said they came under fire and responded in kind. Residents said they felt as if they were under assault by the police, who, they added, fired indiscriminately. . .

The battle now is one of words, with the West Kingston political leaders insisting that the governing party sent in the police to provoke a violent reaction from residents to gain an edge and close their gap in the polls. Violence has long accompanied campaigns here. With parliamentary elections to be held by the end of next year at the latest, the feeling is one of déjà vu.

Former Prime Minister Edward Seaga, a Labor representative from West Kingston in Parliament, said today that despite police talk of guns and criminals lurking in the slums, the police have yet to conduct any searches in Tivoli Gardens. . .

Other people said Mr. Seaga's party exploited the violence, as well, to force early elections. Some people, who had hoped the country was turning away from its history of politically motivated violence, criticized Mr. Seaga for his refusal to meet

63

immediately with Prime Minister P. J. Patterson to help defuse the crisis. . .

The intent of the police action in Tivoli Gardens, Mr. Seaga's supporters said, was to portray it and other Labor strongholds as lawless areas and their leaders as irresponsible.

To many residents of the rickety houses that line the dirty and crumbling streets, it is the governing People's National Party that has failed in its responsibility to look after all citizens, not just those who voted for them.

When a similar sweep and confrontation occurred there in May 1997, Labor's popularity sank in the polls and the People's National Party returned Mr. Patterson to a second term.

The unrest had its beginnings in April, when a community leader allied with the governing party was shot dead. Some people contended that he had been slain by the opposition's supporters. In the next weeks, 17 people were killed in drive-by shootings and other confrontations. Labor supporters insisted that 13 of the dead were party loyalists.

A curfew was already in effect in Tivoli Gardens late last week when the police arrived looking for guns. Residents said they had no warning of what was to follow on Saturday morning.

"The police came down Spanish Town Road and just started firing," said Lorraine Campbell, who owns a beverage stand across the street from the military command post. "They didn't say anything. I closed my shop and ran. . ."

The police said snipers in a housing complex a block away had shot at them. That building's walls are pockmarked with bullet holes. . .

Elsewhere in the neighborhood, people said they had been trapped for days, unable to go out for food or medicine. Labor officials said an 82-year-old diabetic had died because he could not obtain treatment. Others waited until today to go to a community center to pick up food donated by church groups. . .

Excerpted and reprinted with permission,
The New York Times *(July 12, 2001)*

Memo to the West Kingston Commission of Enquiry*f*

In September 2001, Jamaica's prime minister and governor-general named a Commission of Enquiry to examine the series of events that led up to the violent disturbance in West Kingston the weekend of July 7-10 earlier that year (previous chapter and Box 4). The Commission asked me to assist in its work by focussing on three key areas mentioned in its "Terms of Reference." That is, to recommend measures that would contribute to:

- "Permanent and effective solutions for a more peaceful social order in the communities affected".
- "The enhancement of relationships" between the security forces.

f From brief submitted February 5, 2002, to Commission of Enquiry into violent events in West Kingston on July 7-10, 2001.

- "The control and reduction of criminality" within the affected areas.

What follows is a revised text of my report to the Commission.

The Scourge of Violent Crime

The violent events that took place in West Kingston on July 7-10, the after-effects of which would spill over into other areas of the city for another three days, occurred within a broader context of urban violence. A more or less consistent pattern of escalating violent crime and recurring violence had been building steadily over the previous 25 to 30 years.

Official data show that incidents of crime increased steadily, and sometimes dramatically, in the years following political independence, in 1962. In the 1950s through early 1960s, the national murder rate averaged less than six per 100,000 people. By the 1980s it had risen to 23 per 100,000 (Phillips and Wedderburn 1988). Shortly thereafter that rate would be twice as high as that of all major cities in the United States. At the end of 2001 the country's 1,139 murders translated to an incredible 45.5 homicides per 100,000 people, a figure that exceeded all but three countries in the world.

In the weeks and months leading up to the early morning hours of July 7, 2001, stories of violent crimes and partisan-motivated conflicts, occurring within blighted areas of the Kingston Metropolitan Area (KMA), dominated press and television news. They described how violence, and the threat of violence, was limiting access to jobs and schools, and undercutting practically all aspects of community life.

Kingston: Stage for a Non-Peaceful Order

Although crime and violence have not been confined either to Jamaica's urban areas, or to poor people, they have tended "to be geographically concentrated in poor urban communities." (Moser 1997) Within the last 20 years, more than half of the country's violent crimes occurred in Kingston and St. Andrew; and three-quarters of the murders and more than 80 per cent of shootings have taken place in Kingston and its immediate environs.

Kingston emerged as the hub of economic expansion in Jamaica's post-war modernization effort. Economic growth brought rapid urbanisation and rural-urban migration, and Kingston soon became the primate city of Jamaica. The renowned pioneer Jamaican demographer Professor George Roberts (n. d.) calculated the total number of "internal movers of both sexes" to Kingston for the period 1943-60 to have exceeded "the total gross emigration from the island by 32 per cent." The level of capital accumulation in the central city was, however, insufficient to absorb this burgeoning labour force. Unemployment in the areas to which rural residents first settled—notably Western Kingston—ran high. To survive, youthful males in particular had to eke out marginal existences through some combination of casual labour, family support, and an ingenious array of legal and illegal hustles. This non-wage-earning working class has over the years comprised Jamaica's ubiquitous sufferer population.

Politicians of the two major political parties, the Jamaica Labour Party (JLP) and the People's National Party (PNP), would discover in the years following independence that they could entice with political spoils the sufferers in ghetto constituencies; and that, effectively administered, political patronage of the most divisive sort could ensure—in perpetuity—constituents' unwavering loyalties.

"Loyalty" has, though, since the early years of political self-rule, transcended its original terms. It has turned into an insidious force, particularly in areas of mass urban poverty, where it developed into "political tribalism"—a force that, as the Barbadian author George Lamming (1981) put it, "smothers all critical judgement about social and political issues, and makes the ordinary decent citizen afraid of being overheard." Lamming continues: "It is as though members of the political parties see themselves as loyal warriors of two rival tribes, each regarding the other's existence as a threat to his own; and where the tribe that comes to power takes possession of the total political estate, free at last to reward prizes to the most diligent of its henchmen, and to punish by careful exclusion, those whose tribal allegiance lies elsewhere."

Keen observers of the Jamaican political scene have maintained that political tribalism[1] has been, at root, responsible for fomenting much of Kingston's violent history. Signs of this damaging phenomenon emerged, they point out, in the country's first national election after universal adult suffrage in 1944, when loyalists for the JLP and the PNP engaged each other in relatively light, non-anarchical skirmishes; combatants used then mostly fists, stones, and knives. The violence would, however, gain more deadly momentum in the ensuing years.

1948-1966

Partisan-motivated political violence reached crisis level in the months leading up to the second general election after adult suffrage. So much so that page one of *The Daily Gleaner* of May 16, 1948, printed signed statements by JLP Leader Alexander Bustamante and PNP President Norman Manley, both pledging to put an end to the use of force in their political campaigns. "It is wrong to throw stones or other missiles at political meetings, [to] attack, abuse or insult opponents," the statement instructed respective party followers. "Bravo!" exclaimed the edition's front-page editorial.

Political conflict would nonetheless take on a far more earnest—and lethal—quality years later in the period leading up to the nation's first post-independence general election, in 1967. The dominant feature in the new kind of violence was the emergence of rival political gangs whose members had been recruited, directly or indirectly (or their violent activities "winked at"), by politicians and political "kingmakers" (Stone 1980, 1985; Figueroa, 1994).

The gangs' early leaders—the "top ranking"—were drawn from groups of "rude boys" who had been nurtured in an explosive subculture of street crime and violence that had crystallized in the mushrooming urban-ghetto communities. Close links with politicians afforded the top ranking access to work contracts and other political party favours. And close links with the top ranking gave middle class politicians leverage in divisive intra-class struggles that, in the end, would still leave intact the basic political and economic system.

The gangs began operating in the low-income communities of Kingston and South-West St. Andrew. Their main purpose, as related in loosely connected oral histories, was—and still is—to intimidate voters and cement "political garrisons" within select areas.[2] In May 1966, a night-time guerrilla war between rival political top rankings, and their respective disciples, culminated in the country's first State of Emergency.

1967-1980

Major political violence would again erupt in 1976. The conflation of circumstances behind the outbursts then gives an excellent background understanding to all *political* clashes to follow in the succeeding years.

During its ten-year reign, from 1962 to 1972, the JLP succeeded in creating safe seats in the KMA (traditionally a PNP stronghold) through its ambitious low-income housing schemes. They built the Tivoli Gardens housing project on the rot of Back O' Wall in Western Kingston, and Wilton Gardens (what would later become known as "Rema") in South St. Andrew. Work on the construction sites, as well as the allotment of homes, was reserved for JLP supporters. A third housing project, Arnett Gardens, was under construction opposite Wilton Gardens when the JLP suffered defeat at the polls in 1972. The project was completed, but officials within the new PNP government handed over the units to supporters of the area's winning PNP candidate. By the mid-1970s, then, "political victimisation" in the two contiguous constituencies—first from one political side and then the other—had created fiercely opposed sufferer locales. Politically hostile residents were left literally facing down each other.

The cue to renewed violence in 1976 was the start of voter registration in preparation for the pending election. The principal arena for war was South St. Andrew, where armed gangs from "Rema," propped up by Tivoli "shock troops," fought pitched battles against "Jungle" PNP rivals. To stem the violent tide, the PNP government under Michael Manley declared a State of Emergency aimed chiefly at political gunmen. All top ranking known to the Special Branch of the Jamaica Constabulary were placed under "heavy manners" (i.e., temporarily imprisoned).

The psychological impact of the State of Emergency was damaging to the JLP, which the PNP had succeeded in identifying in the public sphere with conspiratorial violence. The widespread view of Edward Seaga, the JLP Member of Parliament for West Kingston who had assumed leadership of the JLP in 1974, as a ruthless, power-hungry politician further undermined the JLP's standing. In December 1976, the electorate voted overwhelmingly to return the incumbent Manley government to power.

1980-1997

Four years following Manley and the PNP's landslide re-election in 1976, the country was to witness its worst case of political violence, when "tangled strands of urban warfare" were "woven into an enormously complex and brutal scenario." (NACLA 1980) The political violence of 1980 reportedly left more than 800 people dead. In predawn attacks, gunmen invaded tenement houses, killing old people, women, and children. "The targeting for extermination of the elderly and young children, almost unfathomable in a culture that reveres its old and shields its young at all costs, and of women, previously excluded from the sphere of violence, marked a critical break with past political warfare," which until then had primarily been a top ranking affair. (NACLA 1980, p. 42) Political gunmen forced the depopulation of Coronation Market, the principal distribution centre for food brought into Kingston from the countryside. Attacks on country buses carrying rural higglers to the urban centre—and shootings in the market vicinity itself—compelled the diversion of produce to outlying markets.

Narrow politically motivated partisan violence subsided in relative terms through the remaining years of the 1980s, and much of the early 1990s—though a sudden rash of violence and "severe election malpractices" marred the 1993 election, according to reputable independent observers. The relative calm of the early 1990s occurred largely as a result of two inter-related developments.

The first was that several top rankings were spirited abroad, reportedly by their political patrons, because they had become inconvenient burdens on a state system of rapidly contracting spoils. The second and perhaps more significant development was that many leading top ranking political gunmen branched out full-time into normal criminal activities, often carrying along with them their rude boy following. Exporting to North America and Europe forbidden Jamaican ganja was one such illegal activity. Then, "when the [JLP] government campaign in 1985 against ganja closed down the business," according to one witness at the Commission hearings, PNP activist Paul Burke, "persons sought to go into cocaine importation."[3]

With the trade in cocaine came a build-up of illegal weapons, especially of high-powered rifles. The business of international narcotics trafficking moreover required many top rankings to relocate to cities in the United States, where, throughout the 1980s, they dominated the illegal drug trade, mostly because of their excessive violent modus operandi.[4] Activities that nominally would have been considered "political violence," then, remained for a time contained—until 1997.

1997-July 2001

The role of politics in violent episodes assumed yet another dimension in 1997, when use of coercive state power by agents of the state, acting at the behest of elected political authority, took on *perceived* political ramifications. The coercive apparatus, namely the army and police, might have in those episodes been directed to carry out a purely law enforcement function—usually to apprehend wanted criminals. But because notable instances of such directives involved seemingly overwhelming or "heavy" enforcement operations directed inside a community staunchly opposed to the ruling regime, residents there—and their elected opposition spokespersons—interpreted the action as partisan inspired state violence, even state "terrorism." That interpretation would appear saliently brought out if an operation turned bloody, with innocent residents losing their lives from police or army action.

Of such would seem at least some of the initial details of what happened on May 1997, in the JLP fortress of Tivoli Gardens, where, for the vast majority of residents, their long-serving Member of Parliament, Opposition Leader Edward Seaga, is a man larger than life, of mythic proportions.

The Daily Gleaner in a number of separate stories captured this latest intersection of politics within a spiralling violent episode. According to one of these stories,

Gunshots rang out for more than 90 minutes in Tivoli Gardens late yesterday [i.e., Tuesday, May 6]. A Jamaica Defence Force (JDF) armoured car was seen in the community and two helicopters were circling. All roads leading into Tivoli Gardens were blocked. Business places drew their shutters, school children and people coming from work had to dash for cover.

Residents who spoke with The Gleaner said that while they were having prayers over the body of Rohan Fraser, who was killed by the police last week, JDF soldiers came and verbally abused them, then started shooting. Fraser's funeral is scheduled for today. The casket with the body had a bullet hole, as did the window of the house. All this, the residents claimed, was done by the soldiers . . .

Member of Parliament Edward Seaga in a release said police and soldiers staged a mass invasion of the Tivoli Gardens community, and without provocation opened fire on residents. This, he said, was witnessed by two teachers from a nearby school. He said that the security forces proceeded to the home where Fraser was shot by police last week. 'The house was shot up by the security forces, the casket with the dead man's body was shot, a female family member was shot . . .'

Reprinted with permission, *The Gleaner.*

Minister of National Security, K. D. Knight, issued a stern warning to the residents that the security forces would be ridding the West Kingston community of drugs, ammunition and guns, in the same way that such missions were carried out in any stronghold of the PNP. (*The Gleaner,* May 8, 1997)

Between May 1997, when this event occurred in Tivoli Gardens, and the general election of December that year, a tense calm existed between West Kingston's JLP enclaves and the PNP government. A similar situation also held between JLP- and PNP-affiliated gangs in adjoining West Kingston and South St. Andrew constituencies. But no major violent clashes occurred. Within weeks following the election, community leaders forged a "peace offensive," which enjoyed the guarded approval of the two members of Parliament representing abutting JLP and PNP constituencies—the JLP's West Kingston, represented by Opposition Leader Edward Seaga; and the PNP's St. Andrew South, represented by Minister of Finance Dr. Omar Davies.

Football matches and other festive occasions regularly brought together people from PNP-dominated Arnett Gardens and the JLP's Tivoli Gardens. This relative peace would last for a full three years—until one afternoon in April 2001, when the gun slaying of three men in Arnett Gardens shattered it all.

Within weeks following the killing of William Moore, Albert Bonner, and Lowell Hinds relations across Western Kingston's political fault lines swiftly returned to their pre-1980s' war days. Moore and Bonner, though known to the police as gangsters,

Youth scurrying across a besieged West Kingston street on the morning of July 7, 2001

were also well-known PNP supporters; Moore having been regarded by the PNP as an "area leader." Their mysterious killing triggered widespread violent reaction across the length and breadth of lower St. Andrew and Western Kingston; much of it directed at presumed JLP constituents in reprisal for specifically Moore's and Bonner's killing.

At least 24 people died in the wake of these attacks, and 798 families were burnt out of their homes. JLP leader Edward Seaga returned to his familiar posture of charging his political opponents with having blood on their hands. "The only thing I can tell the Prime Minister right now is to tell his people to stop the violence," Seaga said on June 11. Men from the PNP enclave of Hannah Town, he said, burnt and destroyed homes of JLP residents in Denham Town.

The violence on the morning of July 7 occurred, therefore, within an historical context of continued tribal political warfare. The police operation might never have commenced that July morning—or the police given a "pretext" for it to commence—had there not been perpetuation of a kind of political practice with roots going back to the earliest stages in the nation's development.[5]

Twenty-four additional people lost their lives that day because, according to security forces officials, they had to go in to stop a war between politically affiliated combatants. That "war"—a fratricidal war between equally suffering Jamaicans who merely supported two different political parties—had been simmering for two long months and was threatening to get even more deadly; a war between forces on the ground whose respective elite leadership, since the general election of February 1989, mirrored each other in national policy objectives and underlying political ideology.

The security forces could thus make the credible claim that they needed to stop the ongoing "political war" in Western Kingston. They had to "go in" to, first, find the guns; then seize and remove them.[6]

I. Recommendations for a Peaceful Order

Given the above formulation, recommendations for creating a more peaceful social order, especially in the communities of interest, fall within short, intermediate, and long-term proposals.

A. For the **short** (i.e., *immediate*) term, I propose that:

R1. *The national government seek immediately to develop partnerships with business and philanthropic organizations to strengthen the resource base of the Ministry of National Security's recently instituted "Peace Management/Social Conflict Intervention Initiative."*

The Peace Initiative has as its objective "setting up of an early warning and intervention mechanism within specific communities [beginning in the Kingston Metropolitan area], which will allow for the early detection and management of potentially explosive, criminal or violent situations in such communities." The Initiative's Terms of Reference call for it to: [a] "Be the focal point for information about potential explosive situations"; [b] "Act as mediator [and facilitator] in the face of potential conflict in community or potentially explosive situations"; [c] "Coordinate community action to pre-empt eruption of violence"; [d] "Provide counselling support for potential perpetrators or victims of crime and/or violence"; [e] "Identify situations which can become explosive and make the necessary referrals to the relevant bodies to immediately defuse these situations"; and [f] "Liaise with other Governmental and Non-Governmental organisations in order to defuse potential for violence."

R2. *Government should solicit international assistance in launching peace centres inside the communities of interest in an immediate effort to help residents reduce the incidence of violence.*
The peace centres ought to be staffed with trained mediators to whom residents can turn for help in settling community disputes and conflicts before they erupt in violence. Other counsellors would assist in matters of grief counselling. One such centre was opened in January 2002 in the Grants Pen community (in North St. Andrew), under sponsorship of the United States Embassy.

The focus is on the national government to initiate these two recommendations, because, first of all, partisan-driven government policies under one ruling regime and then another did much to foster the deterioration in parts of Kingston's inner city. But, also, only the national government has the resources to mobilize for quick-action response to the crisis crime and violence have now become. To civil society will fall the more important function of nurturing and sustaining the response initiatives.

B. For the **intermediate term**, I call the nation's attention, as others have before, to the lists of comprehensive recommendations related to the problem of political tribalism that have been proposed in recent times by distinguished task forces and previous commissions. What's clearly needed is the political will to bring about change.

R3. *Government, political opposition, and relevant civic agencies must now diligently seek to implement the recommendations set forth in the Report of the National Committee on Political Tribalism, the "Kerr Report," as regards changing the situation of political tribalism.*

The following require serious attention:
- "Politicians must not only pay lip service to, but must also become actively involved in the eradication of a political arena where gunslingers establish and operate tribal boundaries."
- "Politicians must divest themselves of the responsibility of issuing scarce benefits and leave the civil servant and impartial committees to implement policies in an objective and unbiased fashion based on set criteria."
- "The distribution of houses, social services or determination of where an industry is sited ought not to be dependent upon whether or not the area sup-

ports the government of the day. The only criteria for the distribution of such benefits should be NEED and VIABILITY" [emphasis supplied].

- "Politicians must begin to get people to understand that involvement in politics is not a prerequisite to receiving the benefits that it is incumbent on Government to provide for its citizens."
- "Members of Parliament representing garrison constituencies or constituencies in which there are areas of political violence must by example, exhortation and rebuke, inculcate political tolerance and respect for the constitutional rights of freedom of association."
- "Political leaders must publicly denounce officers and members who are associated with criminals, political and otherwise, and take disciplinary action to remove from office those found in breach of the terms and ethics of the Peace Agreement" [signed in 1988 and 1993 by the leaders of the JLP and PNP].
- "Political leaders of all levels should disassociate themselves from reputed criminals, in particular those committing crimes of violence or offences in breach of the Representation of the People's Act and kindred laws." (Government of Jamaica 1997, pp. 19-20)

Perhaps implementation and sustained adherence to these pointed recommendations will happen only when the electorate truly holds their elected representatives to a higher standard than the representatives may have grown accustomed to.

C. The most sustainable solutions for any social problem are always for the **long term**. The resort to violence as a method for resolving disputes, differences, and "issues"— political or otherwise—is normal behaviour developed over the course of perhaps several generations. Its reversal can only occur, therefore, over the long haul.

But that will only happen through sustained, generations-long processes of education and re-education. It will require training in methods of conflict resolution. That is, individuals being able to identify and implement solutions to problems in conflict situations; then learning and understanding that the best solutions are those that are non-violent, but still meeting their needs and improve their relationships with others. In general, conflict resolution education programmes provide individuals with the knowledge, skills, abilities, and processes needed to choose alternatives to self-destructive, violent behaviour.

The United States, Canada, and Australia have had noticeable success merging education in conflict resolution methods with **restorative justice**. Such projects ought to be seriously looked at for Jamaica. Restorative justice represents another, or perhaps new, way of thinking about crime. The theories underlying restorative justice suggest more concentrated focus on those most directly affected by crime: the victim, the offender, and the community (Kurki 1999, Van Ness and Strong 1997, Van Ness 1986). Restorative justice is based on the premise that communities will be strengthened if local citizens participate in responding to crime. It also envisions responses tailored to the preferences and needs of victims, communities, and offenders.

The central idea of **restorative justice** is that justice systems should actively engage the parties touched by crime in repairing the injustices caused by crime. This means that individual offenders should indeed be held accountable for having hurt real people, and real communities; and that they should be required to help make their victims (or families of victims) whole again. Making restitution (or reparation) to crime victims is essential to individual rehabilitation, healing and reconciliation, and to restoring a community that had been sundered by a crime, or crimes.

The restorative justice process differs significantly, then, from the retributive idea of justice that underlines criminal justice systems generally. These portrayals of justice differ both in their understanding of crime and their approach to addressing it. Howard Zehr in his influential book on restorative justice, *Changing Lenses: A New Focus for Crime and Justice (1990)*, offers the following helpful comparison between the restorative and retributive understandings of justice (cited in Llewellyn 2002, pp. 9-10):

Retributive Lens	Restorative Lens
Blame-fixing central	Problem-solving central
Focus on past	Focus on future
Needs secondary	Needs primary
Battle model: adversarial	Dialogue normative
Emphasizes differences	Searches for commonalities
Imposition of pain considered normative	Restoration and reparation considered normative

Harm by offender balanced by harm to offender	Harm by offender balanced by making right
Focus on offender; victim ignored	Victims' needs central
State and offender are key elements	Victim and offender are key elements
Victims lack information	Information provided to victims
Restitution rare	Restitution normal
Victims' "truth" secondary	Victims' suffering lamented and acknowledged
Action from state to offender: offender passive	Offender given role in solution
State monopoly on response to wrongdoing	Victim, offender, and community roles recognized
Offender does not have responsibility for resolution	Offender has responsibility in resolution
Outcomes encourage offender irresponsibility	Responsible behaviour encouraged
Rituals of personal denunciation and exclusion	Rituals of lament and re-ordering
Offender denounced	Harmful act denounced
Offender's ties to community weakened	Offender's integration into community increased
Offender seen in fragments	Offender viewed holistically
Sense of balance through retribution	Sense of balance through restitution
Balance righted by lowering offender	Balance righted through restitution
Justice tested by intent and process	Justice tested by its "fruits"
Justice as right rules	Justice as right relationships

Victim-offender relationships ignored	Victim-offender relationships central
Process alienates	Process aims at reconciliation
Response based on offender's past behaviour	Response based on consequences of offender's behaviour
Repentance and forgiveness discouraged	Repentance and forgiveness encouraged
Proxy professions are the key actors	Victim and offender central; professional help available
Competitive, individualistic values encouraged	Mutuality and cooperation encouraged
Ignores social, economic, and moral context of behaviour	Total context relevant
Assumes win-lose outcomes	Makes possible win-win outcomes

I see the ideals of restorative justice as essential to restoring peace and healing to the communities affected by the violent events of July 7-10. Individuals in, say, Tivoli Gardens, who may have done harm to others in, say, "Rema" or Hannah Town (or vice versa) should be encouraged to meet one another (with available professional assistance) in a restorative process. A key first step, though, would be for rival politicians to do the same, followed by a series of restorative dialogues between the security forces (police and army) and residents of the affected communities.

Along these lines I offer, then, two specific recommendations:

R4. *In conjunction with the short- and intermediate-term recommendations put forward earlier, government,*

*business, and philanthropic organizations must dem-
onstrate firm, **long-term** commitment—through funding and other support—to agencies in the society that
have implemented peaceful conflict-resolution strategies.*

R5.*The Jamaica government (particularly the Department of Corrections) should work with philanthropic
and faith-based organizations to implement restorative justice projects in the communities of interest.*

I site as regards R4 and R5 the closely related, ongoing
work of two agencies—PALS Jamaica and The Dispute Resolution Foundation.

"PALS is a non-profit foundation dedicated to changing
attitudes towards violence and to promoting conflict resolution in the Jamaican society. The letters PALS stand for Peace
and Love in Schools." (PALS Jamaica n. d., p. 7) The PALS
programme is offered primarily to teachers in primary or el-
ementary schools, and more recently to a limited number of
high schools. However, parental involvement in, and support
for, the programme is critical; it is therefore courted and encouraged. The programme trains teachers in the knowledge
and skills of conflict resolution, which the teachers are in turn
expected to pass on to their students. The PALS curricula
provide step-by-step instruction for training in mediation and
for monitoring participants' progress.

An independent evaluation of PALS conducted in August
2000 reports: "The findings of our assessment indicate that

the PALS programme has had a positive impact on the target groups and communities in which it has been introduced. Some of the observed results of the Programme include a positive effect in behaviours of school children, improvement in classroom behaviour, strong community support for PALS and significant impact on parent behaviours in, and attendance at, parent-teachers meetings. It is clear that the programme has had a significant level of success in achieving its objectives of reducing violence in the school system, and implementing effective conflict resolution techniques." (Global Associates Ltd. 2000, p. 2)

The PALS programme is currently being implemented in 300 primary schools representing a population of approximately 160,000 students. PALS' ultimate success, supporters believe, will be measured in the kind of attitudes and the quality of the behaviours of the adults in society who graduated from its curriculum. PALS was given favourable, "thumbs-up" mention by the Member of Parliament, Omar Davies, for its positive impact in his constituency—one of the communities of interest to the Commission. For this, along with the favourable empirical assessments highlighted above, I urge full support for its efforts.

The Dispute Resolution Foundation (DRF), formerly the Mediation Council of Jamaica, was incorporated under the Companies Act in July 1994. Core funding was provided by USAID under the Sustainable Justice Improvement Programme. The Foundation seeks to implement, through collaborative efforts with key stakeholder agencies like PALS, models of dispute resolution at the grassroots.

The DRF's main objectives are:

- To establish methods—Alternative Dispute Resolution (ADR) techniques—of resolving disputes that supplement, or are alternatives to, litigation

- To encourage and educate the public about using ADR techniques to handle conflicts and differences without resorting to violence

- To establish dispute resolution facilities in communities throughout Jamaica

- To explore and establish ADR techniques as methods of resolving domestic, commercial, industrial, political, and social disputes.

These core objectives the DRF seeks to realize through intensive training (with emphases on simulation and role playing) of counsellors in its mediation techniques. Mediation for the Foundation "is not simply sitting around and talking about a problem. Mediation is organized negotiation. It is a structured process in which the mediator guides the disputants through a discussion of their mutual problems and concerns, organises the parties' presentations of alternatives for resolving the problem and aids the parties in arriving at a resolution of their dispute." (DRF Handout)

The DRF, despite its useful work, particularly as a support agency for the country's crowded court system, is one of those civic agencies to which, as one of its directors put it, the Jamaican government has given only "lip service." It is severely under funded and under staffed. Thus it is, more often than not, unable to keep up with the routine demands placed on it—including disputants in need of assistance walking in off the street to its main centre. An essential for a new peaceful order will be heightened commitment to the viability of the Dispute Resolution Foundation and the projects it undertakes.

II. Improving Structurally the Relationship with the Police

One reason for the recorded dramatic decreases in violent crime in the United Sates in the 1990s was the sustained effort of the federal government to involve and engage communities—working with law enforcement—in strategies for crime prevention. The most effective of these measures was reorganization of both large and small police departments so that its beat officers could return (as they did in a bygone era) to fundamentals of community policing.

Community policing is a philosophy of policing. It is based on the concept that police officers and private citizens working together in creative ways can help solve contemporary community problems related to crime, fear of crime, social and physical disorder, and neighbourhood decay (Trojanowicz and Bucqueroux 1990). The philosophy is predicated on the belief that achieving these goals will require police agencies to develop new relationships with the law-abiding people in the community, allowing them a greater voice in setting local police priorities, and involving them in efforts to improve the overall quality of life in their neighbourhoods.

Essential to community policing are two critical departures from traditional policing. First is that community policing shifts the focus of police work from handling random and crisis calls to *solving community problems*. Community policing goes beyond problem-oriented policing to include problem-solving approaches. Problem-oriented policing rightfully recognizes the benefits of involving the police directly in the community.

Take, for instance, the traditional call and police response to the crime of robbery at a particular bus or taxi stand. In normal or traditional policing, the way this incident is handled is that, for example, the Hunt's Bay police station eventually gets the call for service, naturally after the crime has been committed. By the time the police officer arrives on the scene, s/he usually does little more than take a report, since the culprits have been long gone.

We might improve that wasteful situation with a problem-oriented approach. A technique like crime-mapping or crime analysis would flag the department to the persistent problems at that particular stand. An officer skilled in problem-oriented policing would investigate why that particular stand has so many robberies. He would likely suggest one basic solution: remove the stand or change it to a different location, without really checking back to see if that had solved the problem.

If no more robberies were reported from that location, the officer would have reason to feel confident that the problem had indeed been solved. But that would depend on people not calling to report any more robberies at that location.

Community policing, which emphasizes both problem-oriented and problem-solving approaches, would approach that same situation differently. An officer trained in the methods and approaches of community policing—a community policing officer (CPO)—assigned on foot-patrol to that area might very well have uncovered the problem on her own, rather than to have it flagged to her attention by headquarters. In fact, a CPO might well discover problems headquarters never did, since many victims never report crimes to the police.

A CPO might employ the same problem-solving tactics to our robbery example: having the taxi stand removed. But her presence in the community would also allow her to find out whether that solution actually worked.

The second departure is more challenging: *community policing is power sharing.* A community policing agenda is influenced by the community's needs and desires, not just the dictates of the police or national security apparatus. It provides a *quid pro quo*. The community-policing officer says to people in the beat area: If you provide information and assistance to us, you will in exchange receive an opportunity to have input into the police priorities in your community.

This empowers citizens. But empowering average citizens also requires an important adjustment in the line officer's thinking. Traditional officers who believe their authority and police uniform should be sufficient to demand compliance (as in *come ya to mi bwai*) may find it difficult to make the shift to sharing power demanded by community policing.

All things considered, I suggest that implementation of community policing in any area of Jamaica is less a problem of logistics and infrastructure than of institutional change, and of resistance to change. Nothing I have described here is impossible for, or in the long run unworkable in, inner city Kingston. But change always threatens traditional institutional arrangements and comfort zones. And the more dramatic and far-reaching the change, the more it will be resisted by those who see themselves as having the most to lose.

I nonetheless recommend that, as a solid indication that the government and its policing agencies intend to change structurally the relationship between the police/security forces and residents of the inner city, it should:

> **R6.** *Put in on the ground in West Kingston, as suggested in the Police Executive Research Forum (PERF 2001) report to the Jamaican government, a bona fide pilot community-policing project. The project should be developed with the philosophy and ideals stipulated above, and along operational lines that have been successfully implemented in other parts of the world.*

III.   Control and Reduction of Criminality

Several academic studies of and task force reports on the root causes of crime and violence in Jamaica have been published over the last 20 or more years (see, e.g., Bibliography in *Crime, Peace and Justice In Jamaica: A Transformative Approach* [University of the West Indies, Mona, 2001]). The causes that have been identified can be grouped as follows:

> ✓ Culture of aggressiveness if not always clearly a culture of violence. This is borne out by the high number of domestic and reprisal killings, glorification (par-

ticularly among the urban poor) of the "bad man" hero,
· and the reflexive tendency across all sectors of the
society to act aggressively, to "never back down."

✓ The disproportionately large number of people who
exist in disorganized slum conditions that hamper development of constructive family relations, breed low
self-esteem, and impede a sense of community.

✓ The void created by absence of community being filled
over time not by "repairers of the breach," but by as-
sorted charlatans and destroyers who have sought to
gain political and other gains through sanctioning
more crime, bloodshed, and suffering.

✓ The frustrations of trying to achieve and to survive,
through culturally approved means e.g., a job, steady
employment or entrepreneurship.

Based on the foregoing conclusions about the causes of
crime in the Jamaican society, a number of recommendations for reducing its levels have equally been voluminously
put to the Jamaican government and people. I recommend
that,

R7. *Political and civic leadership re-emphasize to the na-
tion the need to implement the crime reduction pro-
posals offered in, for example, Report of The National
Task Force on Crime, the so-called "Wolfe Report"
(Government of Jamaica 1993); the document,
Crime, Peace and Social Justice: A Transformative
Approach (ibid); and the Report of the National Com-
mittee on Crime (Government of Jamaica 2001).*

The last is not only the most recent, but also the most far-reaching in its list of 16 recommendations, which the Report summarizes as follows:

1) The political leadership in the country must recommit to a set of values and a code of conduct consistent with the vision of a safe, peaceful and prosperous Jamaica.

2) Inculcate proper values and attitudes in the youth of Jamaica . . .

3) Strengthen parenting skills, particularly for children at risk to violence.

4) Empower communities to effectively participate in the judicial process . . .

5) Leverage positive school/community relationship to address the problem of crime and violence.

6) Empower communities to plan their best possible future and to solve their problems. . .

7) Re-establish/strengthen legitimate leadership within communities and break the cycle of political patronage.

8) (a) Bring the private sector into active partnership with communities through a national adopt-a-community programme.

   (b) Network/twin communities to combine strengths and to avert the current trend towards a divided society.

(c) Give troubled communities an opportunity for a fresh start.

9) (a) Bring in the guns. . .

(b) Stop the flow of guns into the country . . .

10) Improve police effectiveness and community policing relationship. . .

11) Utilize reformed gang leaders in the fight against crime and violence.

12. Develop special legislation to address acts of terrorism.

13. (a) Introduce affirmative action in employment.

(b) Increase levels of employment in poor communities.

(c) Rehabilitate infrastructure and housing in marginal communities.

14. (a) Eliminate political tribalism.

(b) Develop job descriptions for parliamentarians.

(c) Eliminate persons with questionable backgrounds and connections from representational politics.

15. Change method of appointing members to the Police Services Commission to reflect more of a bipartisan approach.

16. Adopt bipartisan approach to addressing crime and violence.

Conclusion

In the end, mobilising national resources and bending international goodwill to fight "narco-terrorists" in Jamaica not only misses the mark: it's a war against a non-existent enemy, like dogs barking at shadows in the dark. Peace came eventually to Central America when ruling regimes there sat down and negotiated with the region's "terrorist" organizations, including finding ways to include them in national elections. The same will have to happen—and is in a sense happening, despite many stops and starts—in Columbia (Box 3), Peru, and Northern Ireland.

This is unlikely to occur with Jamaica's drug posses and their overlords, simply because they are not terrorists motivated by abstruse political ends. They have no cause. Some are seduced by the semiotics of revolutionary Rastafarianism—especially its rhetorical disdain of the police. But that's as far it goes. Many are motivated by the terrible human condition called greed. Others are driven to seek survival by extraordinarily desperate means. Indeed, posse members working the streets, and drug dons in their fancy automobiles, come from a population of alienated youth who, if nothing else, are fearlessly enterprising. They would move into the heart of Wall Street, Hollywood, or Piccadilly—if they thought there were markets there for them—kidnapped windshield washers from off the corner of Hope and Waterloo Roads.

Continuously reproducing desperate populations that are ready-made "candidates" for murder and mayhem is really the nub of the nation's crime problem. The search for meaningful solutions ought not to lie therefore in the nature of a particular offence, but in the way offenders are nurtured.

Notes

Chapter 1

1. Dons are central figures in the cultural and political
   enigma that are the Kingston inner-city areas. But they
   also figure, though perhaps less dramatically, in the larger
   Jamaican setting. One type of don is an urban community or "area leader," someone who among other things
   is the eyes and ears, the organizer and peacemaker for a
   community's non-resident representative to Parliament.
   Another is the powerful political patron and respectable
   insider with cash and giveaways to spare; the source, or
   sources, of his enormous wealth arrived at "overnight"
   and without detailed paper trail. Still yet another kind of
   don is one who heads a street (or gully) gang involved in
   robbery, burglary, mugging, gunrunning, and direct movement of drugs. This don shares with an appreciative
   ghetto community the fruits of his exploits. He may also
   be simultaneously aligned with a political representative,
   or closely associated with one or the other of the two main

rival political parties. All three types arrive at their respective statuses through widely known reputations of toughness, street savvy, and typically a willingness to use, and prevail at, violence.

Chapter 6

1. One example of exoneration of the state in appalling action in which it had been implicated was the finding of a Commission of Enquiry appointed to look into the Summer 1999 late-night forcible removal of a truckload of street people from the tourist capital of Montego Bay. The victims were bound and blindfolded before being deposited on the edge of a mud lake several miles away in the parish of St. Elizabeth. Local government higher-ups and representatives from the city's business elite were reliably implicated in that scandal. Yet the Commission of Enquiry ended up pinning blame for the entire sordid operation on a lowly female police officer.

2. In a seemingly victorious comeuppance, lawyers for the JLP successfully persuaded fearful residents that it would *not* be in their best interests to give sworn testimony (beyond a preliminary written statement) to the West Kingston Commission of Enquiry.

Chapter 7

1. The Report of the National Committee on Political Tribalism (1997, p. 5) in Jamaica recalls political tribalism being a type of politics known to the ancient Greeks and Romans. "It is political because the tribal grouping is not

ethnic but based upon politics. In a tribe, members of the group and persons within the tribal confines must obsequiously obey and observe the rules and rituals of a tribe or suffer the consequences for disobedience and dissent, so in like manner political tribalism demands unswerving support for a particular political party by persons within the tribal area or suffer the consequences. Thus, political tribalism is the antithesis of our [meaning Jamaican] constitutional democracy, with its freedom of association and the incidental right of the citizen at will to join or support the party of choice."

2. The noted political sociologist, Carl Stone, is credited with introducing the term "garrison" into the political science literature (1985, 1992). "A garrison as the name suggests is a veritable fortress where the dominant [political] party and/or its local agents/supporters are able to exercise control over all significant political, economic and community related social activities." (Figueroa 2000, p. 2) Within the political constituencies defined as garrisons, Figueroa (1985) has identified a consistent pattern of homogeneous voting, even "over-voting," for one party or candidate. Observers from The Carter Center concluded that garrison constituencies are a "socio-economic and political phenomenon unique to Jamaica." (Quoted in Figueroa 2000)

3. Among known top rankings (or "dons," as they would be called in later years) spirited abroad during this period— or who were at least enabled to operate criminal networks

there—was Arnett Gardens drug dealer Anthony Welch, whom news reports say was close to PNP Housing Minister Anthony Spaulding. So also was Tivoli Gardens-based posse boss Lester Lloyd Coke (a.k.a. "Jim Brown"), whose funeral in 1992 JLP leader Edward Seaga attended. Along the funeral cortege route through the streets of West Kingston Seaga chided reporters for not appreciating that Coke was a "protector of his community."

4. In 1987 and 1988, close to 400 homicides committed in the United States were attributed by American authorities to Jamaican "posses." A January 1988 *U.S. News & World Report* story on the problem of the resurgence, in the 1980s, of ethnic gangs in America stated: " Police and prosecutor are puzzled, and in some cases awe-struck, by the sophistication in the Asian gangs, but they are positively alarmed at the propensity for violence of Jamaican criminals." (Quoted in Headley 1996, p. 4)

5. This notwithstanding individuals within the police command structure, notably Senior Superintendent Reneto Adams, head of the Crime Management Unit and officer-in-charge of operations on the morning of July 7, testifying to the West Kingston Commission of Enquiry that the security forces went into the affected areas *after* learning that "a major shipment" of drugs and guns was slated to arrive there.

6. This is not to say that the only, or essential, cause of the violence leading up to and after the morning of July 7 was politics, to the exclusion of all other causes. Cer-

tainly, factors other than politics explain the high levels of crime and violence in the Jamaican society. And it is equally true that many conventional criminals going about their own individual criminal agendas, oblivious to party issues, live and move about within the confines of political garrisons. True also is that criminal gunmen with declared party allegiances have from time to time crossed party tribal lines to form a common fighting front against the police.

Bibliography

Figueroa, M. (2000). Homogeneous Voting, Electoral Manipulation and the Garrison Process in Jamaica, 1962-1993. Presented symposium on "Democracy and Democratisation in Jamaica: Fifty Years of Adult Suffrage," University of the West Indies (UWI), Mona, Jamaica.

_____ (1985). "An Assessment of Over-voting in Jamaica," *Social and Economic Studies* 34 (September), pp. 71-106.

Global Associates Ltd. (2000). Report: Institutional Assessment of Peace and Love in Schools (PALS). Kingston, Jamaica.

Government of Jamaica (2001). Report of the National Committee on Crime and Violence (October).

_____ (1997). Report of The National Committee on Political Tribalism.

_____ (1993). Report of the National Task Force on Crime.

Hariott, A. (2000). Police and Crime Control in Jamaica. Mona: University of the West Indies Press.

Headley, B. (2002). "Narco-terrorism Misses the Mark," *The Sunday Gleaner* (January 20).

_____ (2001). "Community Policing: What it is not, what it is." http://www.jamaicansforjustice.org

_____ (1996). *The Jamaican Crime Scene: A Perspective.* Washington, D.C.: Howard University Press.

_____ (1982). Structural Correlates of Dependent Capitalist Development and Increase in Criminality in Jamaica. Ph.D. dissertation. Washington, D. C.: Howard University.

Inciardi, J. (1988). "Narcoterrorism: A Perspective and Commentary." Presented Annual Meeting of the Academy of Criminal Justice Sciences, San Francisco, California (April).

Jones, E. (1978). "The Political Uses of Enquiry (2): The Post-Colonial Jamaican Context," *Social and Economic Studies* 27 (No. 3): 284-312.

Kurki, L. (1999). *Incorporating Restorative Justice and Community Justice Into American Sentencing and Corrections.* Rockville: National Institute of Justice.

Lacey, T. (1977). *Violence and Politics in Jamaica, 1960-1970.* Totowa, N. J.: Frank Cass.

Llewellyn, J. (2002). Building, Strengthening and Transforming Communities: Exploring the Possibilities for Restorative Justice in Jamaica. Submission to Commission of Enquiry into violent events in West Kingston on July 7-10, 2001. Kingston, Jamaica (January).

North American Congress on Latin America (NACLA): Report on the Americas XIV (1980). "Jamaica: Roots of Electoral Violence," pp. 36-42.

PALS Jamaica (n. d.) Foundation Report.

Phillips, P. and Wedderburn, J. (1988), eds. *Crime and Violence: Causes and Solutions*. Department of Government, UWI, Mona.

Police Executive Research Forum [PERF] (2001). Violent Crime and Murder Reduction in Kingston: Executive Summary and Strategies. Washington, D.C. (February).

Lamming, G. (1981). "On Growing Party Tribalism in Barbados." *Caribbean Contact* 9 (October).

Roberts, G. W. (n. d.) *Provisional Assessment of Growth of the Kingston-St. Andrew Area,* 1960-70. UWI, Mona: ISER.

Scott, P. (2001). "Sacred Battles," *The New York Times Magazine* (September 30).

Statistical Department, Commissioner's Office (2002). Periodic Reports (January).

Stone, C. (1985). *Class, State and Democracy in Jamaica*. Kingston: Blackett.

_____ (1980). *Democracy and Clientelism in Jamaica*. New Brunswick: Transaction.

The Gleaner (2001) "Phillips Urges Unity Against Narco Threat" (November 23).

_____ (2001) "'Cold-blooded Murder'—Bar Council Cites Possibility in Braeton killings" (March 22).

_____ (2001) "Adams on Leave—'Pondering Future' in Wake of Breaton Shootings" (March 16).

_____ (1997) "Child Dies; Mourners Flee, Many 'Trapped'" (May 8).

The Jamaica Observer (2001). "Strong Backing For Adams (December 2).

Trojanowicz, R. and Bucqueroux, B. (1990). *Community Policing: A Community Perspective.* Cincinnati: Anderson Publishing.

University of the West Indies (UWI), Mona (2001). Crime, Peace and Justice in Jamaica: A Transformative Approach.

Van Ness, D. and Strong, K. H. (1997). *Restoring Justice.* Cincinnati: Anderson.

Van Ness, D. (1986). *Crime And Its Victims.* Downers Grove, IL: InterVarsity.

Williams, L. (2001). "The Guns Keep Coming in," *The Gleaner* (November 9).

Zehr, H. (1990). *Changing Lenses: A New Focus for Criminal Justice.* Ontario: Herald.

BETWEEN THE CRACK[f]

Tonight as I lay me down to sleep,
I pray the Lord my life to keep.
The night was cold- the darkness black
But then a stream of light came in – through the crack.

And as I lay there, I remembered home
And all the places I used to roam
The nights when I would always come back
And huddle in my corner of the room
Feeling the breeze coming at me – through the crack.

I remembered school too – although I didn't attend much
But I recall how I'd always yearn for a touch
Hoping that teacher would give me a hug too, a pat on the back.
But I was always ignored seem to get lost – between the crack.

I remember the times I would ask about my father
But would only succeed in making an enemy of my mother.
And as usual her physical and verbal attack,
Would cause me to withdraw like an insect – into a crack.

And so I decided I've got to get tough,
For it was clear to me that my life was going to be very rough.
I was tired of the rejection – tired of the lack
Why should I always be ignored
        – Get lost – between the crack.

But one fateful day I lost my mind
I was hoping to get ahead but instead was left behind.
I entered the drug ring and couldn't turn back
I got deeper – Got busted and was finally put – into this great big crack.

So here I am in this dreadful place
Those who knew me would not even recognize my face
I've been abandoned – my relatives have not come back
I guess, for them its better if I remain here – between the crack.

And now that I have told my story to you
There's something I need to ask you to do,
Make sure when you leave here, when you get back
Go search for and rescue those who have gotten lost –
somehow, somewhere between the crack.

Etta A. Barclay
University of the West Indies
Mona, Jamaica
April 5, 2001

---

[f]Printed with author's permission

Index

About the Author

BERNARD HEADLEY is Professor of Sociology and Criminology in the Faculty of Social Sciences, University of the West Indies, Mona, Jamaica; and Professor Emeritus, Northeastern Illinois University in Chicago, where he taught courses in criminology and criminal justice from 1983 to 2001. A two-time Senior Fulbright Scholar, his other academic works include *The Jamaican Crime Scene: A Perspective* and *The Atlanta Youth Murders and the Politics of Race*. Headley graduated from West Indies College (now Northern Caribbean University) in Mandeville, Jamaica and completed his undergraduate degree at Andrews University in Michigan, USA. He holds a M.A. and Ph.D. in Sociology from Howard University in Washington, D.C. He is currently working on a scholarly biography of Jamaica Labour Party and Opposition Leader, and former Jamaican Prime Minister, Edward Seaga.